Spoon River Anthology

Spoon River Anthology

Edgar Lee Masters

Edited by John Ridland

ET REMOTISSIMA PROPE

Hesperus Poetry

Hesperus Poetry
Published by Hesperus Press Limited
4 Rickett Street, London SW6 1RU
www.hesperuspress.com

Spoon River Anthology first published in 1915
First published by Hesperus Press Limited, 2005

Foreword © Shena Mackay, 2005
Introduction © John Ridland, 2005

Designed and typeset by Fraser Muggeridge
Printed in Jordan by Jordan National Press

ISBN: 1-84391-108-6

CONTENTS

FOREWORD

A funeral is often the starting point of a novel or film, where the black-clothed mourners, the tolling bell, the minister's valediction, all set the scene for revelations to come. Edgar Lee Masters takes this an imaginative step further. What a brilliant story-telling device is his method of letting the dead speak for themselves and in so doing, create the portrait of a community. It is one any novelist burdened with the minutiae of narrative, the getting of characters from A to B and year to year, might envy. There is material for many novels in the 214 free-verse monologues, the tiny autobiographies, which form the text. To take as a model Mackail's *Select Epigrams from the Greek Anthology* was an inspiration; as Martin Seymour-Smith, in his *Guide to Modern World Literature*, has said, the work 'acted as the catalyst required to manufacture the acid of his genius, compounded of an innate bitterness, a passion for the truth, and a rare sympathy for human beings'.

It is possible to feel an affinity with a work of art without actually seeing or hearing it. I was conscious of *Spoon River Anthology* long before I discovered that it did not consist of selected verses by a riparian school of poets. The attraction lay in the name which suggests a silvery handle of water widening into a bowl, a green rushy stretch where white spoonbills waded. When I read the poems, having encountered already many of the prose writers who were Masters' direct heirs, they triggered thoughts of Tennessee Williams, that champion of the doomed, the fragile, the fugitive kind, memories of *Peyton Place*, *Under Milk Wood*, and Stanley Spencer's *Resurrections*.

They cannot heave up the turfs and slabs which entomb them, or embrace in reconciliation like figures in the paintings, but those 'sleeping on the hill' are as vivid, sentient and human. They mock or find comfort in the epitaphs chiselled on their gravestones, contemplate the shattered harp or open book carved there; some burn with old wrongs and resentments while others have the last laugh; some never left Spoon River, and others are foreigners or have returned from abroad to be buried there. There they lie, soldiers, suicides, murderers and victims, the scholars, poets, artists and craftsmen, musicians, teachers, children, atheists and clergy, the corrupt judiciary, the banker and his son who ruined many fellow-citizens, the yearning woman comparing herself to the unwatered geranium withering on her grave. The sweep of history takes in people who remember Abraham Lincoln, and exponents of the new art of photography.

This is the Protestant cemetery, although it houses one dissolute Catholic spurned by his own church (elsewhere an admirable priest is remembered fondly), as well as the Jewish victim of mistaken identity, forced to be here instead of in the Hebrew cemetery in Chicago. One of the saddest exiles is the Confucian Yee Bow, killed casually by a minister's son, who laments that he will never sleep with his ancestors in Peking or see children honouring his own grave. One black man speaks – Shack Dye the blacksmith – who voices his contempt for the ignorant white men who treated him as a buffoon.

Spoon River Anthology is a mosaic or a jigsaw puzzle which takes shape as one finds the interlocking pieces. The tragic story of Minerva Jones, the self-styled 'village poetess', exemplifies, with consummate irony and pathos, the way Masters builds up the picture. Minerva tells how she was 'hooted at, jeered at by the Yahoos of the street, for my heavy body, cock-eye and rolling walk'. One of those Yahoos, 'Butch' Weldy, raped her after a 'brutal hunt'. She turned to Dr Meyers to help with the resulting pregnancy, but she died. Minerva's last, heartbreaking, words are:

> *Will someone go to the village newspaper*
> *And gather into a book the verses I wrote? –*
> *I thirsted so for love!*
> *I hungered so for life!*

There is no hope that posterity will deal more kindly with her than with the Revd Abner Peet, whose sermons were burned as wastepaper after his death.

Now Minerva's father, 'Indignation' Jones, a broken man with matted hair and beard and ragged clothes which belie the fact that he was an educated man from good Welsh stock and boasts blood purer than that of the 'white trash' here, mourns his daughter, tormented and driven to death. Whereafter, he 'crept, crept like a snail through the days / Of my life. / …Going to the grocery store for a little corn meal / And a nickel's-worth of bacon'.

As for 'Butch' Weldy, the whirligig of time brought in its revenges, but not before Butch drunkenly caused the death of Blind Jack the Fiddler. 'Butch' got religion, and appears again as foreman of the jury when Roy Butler faced a trumped-up rape charge. But 'Butch' was to be horribly maimed by an exploding tank of gasoline while working in the canning factory and, blind as Jack the Fiddler, cheated out of his compensation.

Next comes Dr Meyers, loved and respected until the night Minerva came crying to him in her trouble:

> *I tried to help her out – she died –*
> *They indicted me, the newspapers disgraced me,*
> *My wife perished of a broken heart,*
> *And pneumonia finished me.*

Mrs Meyers concludes that her husband's protestations that he was not responsible for Minerva's fall were vain because he, 'poor soul so sunk in sin', had broken both divine and human laws.

Later, when it seems that Mrs Meyers has had the last word, up speaks Willie Metcalfe:

> *They used to call me 'Dr Meyers',*
> *Because, they said, I looked like him.*
> *And he was my father according to Jack McGuire.*

And so the story of Spoon River goes on, rejecting the easy consolation that the dead rest in peace, which a walk in a country churchyard might give. Masters has a 'rare sympathy' with women, from unfulfilled writer to the indomitable and cynical reprobate to the sensual 'lady with delicate tastes' tied to a husband whose breath smells of whiskey and onions. He, poignantly, lies buried with the bony nose of his dog snuggled under his chin. It is Masters' even-handedness in telling not just both but many sides of the story which gives the *Anthology* much of its power as its assorted unquiet souls evoke the streets and surrounding landscape of their quintessentially American town, whose influence has been wider and deeper than they could ever have imagined.

– Shena Mackay, 2005

A librarian friend tells me *Spoon River Anthology* was the first real piece of literature she ever bought with her babysitting money: 'I was in seventh grade and those musings from the grave were just magical to me.' And she was not alone. Since *Spoon River* was published in 1915 it has been published in well over seventy American editions, translated into about twenty other languages, adapted for the stage, and performed as an opera at La Scala. The reasons for this popularity and accessi-bility are easy to see. All the elements that would appeal to twelve year olds are in it (Willis Barnstone has likened Masters to 'an arrested adolescent'): not only outrage at social injustices, lurid scandals and shameful cover-ups, whether sexual, criminal, financial, marital or professional (the banker Thomas Rhodes – also pictured as 'A.D. Blood' and 'Henry Phipps' – smirks Iago-like over villainies which twenty others mention), but also high-flying idealism ('Elijah Browning') and nostalgia for the innocence of childhood ('Hare Drummer'). As its prefatory poem, 'The Hill', makes clear, this book will be a collection of their own epitaphs spoken by the residents of a cemetery in Spoon River, a small community in what politicians like to call the Heartland of America, and the general impression they will leave is that the heart is rotting at the core. These are mostly 'thin, baffled, sour lives kept from full knowledge of themselves and others by false allegiances, ignorance, and bigotry', and caught in 'the interplay of materialism and idealism in a Midwestern town', the poet-critic Louise Bogan wrote in 1951, a year after Masters died.

All this is juicy matter for translators and the style must make it even juicier: no rhyme or even meter to bother about, not much metaphor, few awkward colloquial idioms, plenty of accessible references (the present edition's endnotes explain some out-of-the-way examples). The style of Masters' epitaph speakers is plain and matter-of-fact, derived from J.W. Mackail's prose renderings of *Epigrams from the Greek Anthology*, and they probably lose less in translation than the more complex verse being written by his contemporaries, Robert Frost and Edwin Arlington Robinson. The poet May Swenson heard their voices testifying 'as if on a metaphorical witness stand', where they would have sworn to tell the truth, the whole truth, and nothing but the truth.

Masters himself called *Spoon River Anthology* 'the most preposterous title known to the realm of books', and he had a point. The word 'Anthology' must then still have implied something of the Glory that was Greece and the Grandeur that was Rome, while 'Spoon River' sounds so ungainly you have to check a detailed map of Illinois to determine it is not entirely fictitious – it's not a town, but is a real river. Juxtaposed, they sound like a joke.

Born in 1868, only three years after the Civil War, Edgar Lee Masters grew up in the watershed of the Illinois River in two towns, Lewiston and Petersburg, on its unimpressive tributaries, the Spoon and the Sangamon. His first home was near New Salem, where the young Abe Lincoln had failed as a shopkeeper. (Three hundred miles west, in Kansas City, Missouri, Harry Truman would fail as a haberdasher in 1922, and they weren't the only American Presidents with unimpressive business résumés.)

Masters, a polemical Democrat, later wrote a hostile 'Copperhead' biography of Lincoln, a Republican, who had lost a lawsuit for one of his ancestors. He himself, by contrast, had made a considerable success of a law career, as we might deduce from the unusual number of judges, lawyers, victims and perpetrators populating his cemetery. One of his partners was the formidable Clarence Darrow, who, in a highly publicised 1925 trial, which he lost, defended John Scopes for illegally teaching Evolution in a Tennessee high school. Before that, Darrow had represented Masters' first wife in their bitterly adversarial divorce case, which was also well publicised. Helen took her husband completely to the cleaners, as a result of which Masters wrote book after unsuccessful book to the end of his life trying to keep his head above water.

In 1915 he had been earning and spending over $25,000 a year (more than ten times that in today's dollars), living in a large house with Helen, three children, an automobile and chauffeur, and three other servants. He would lock himself away from the family at night, writing an even dozen books – essays and plays, and poems highly derivative of late nineteenth-century modes and tiresomely regular in their traditional prosody – which he self-published. He satirised his earlier forms in 'Petit, the Poet' – 'Tick, tick, tick, what little iambics / While Homer and Whitman roared in the pines' – but ironically he returned to them after exhausting his vein of free verse in *Spoon River* and its copy-cat sequel *The New Spoon River*.

Luckily, the earlier books attracted little notice. In order not to damage his standing as a lawyer by being tarred and feathered as a poet, Masters had published them under the pseudonym of 'Webster Ford', combining the surnames of the two Jacobean playwrights. Largely an autodidact, Masters had read widely, loved the Ancient Greeks above all, but also admired the writers of the English Renaissance. In Whit Burnett's 1942 collection, *This Is My Best* ('America's 93 Greatest Living Authors present over 150 self-chosen complete masterpieces'), he contributed a twelve-page, quasi-Shakespearean monologue in which the Bard of Avon complains about life to Ben Jonson and Michael Drayton. Perhaps Masters meant to challenge Edwin Arlington Robinson's 1916 monologue on a similar theme, 'Ben Jonson Entertains a Man from Stratford', but it falls short of that as a poem, as it does of the best *Spoon River* epitaphs, suggesting that Masters did not know where his true strength lay.

Spoon River was published in the same year as new volumes by Robinson, Thomas Hardy, and Robert Frost (*North of Boston*). These four books, with some fifty others, were reviewed by William Stanley Braithwaite in his prestigious *Anthology of Magazine Verse for 1915 and Year Book of American Poetry*. (Hardy's poems he underestimated, like many other critics, as 'hewed rather than modelled', explaining, 'Perhaps no man had more to overcome in his own nature in the attempt to write poetry than this great novelist.') Braithwaite envisioned the United States as entering a 'wonderfully poetic period', placing ten poets and more 'on the crown of Parnassus'. Among some lesser and forgotten names were Frost and Masters, but 'on the topmost peak' Braithwaite set 'the silent and lordly figure' of E.A. Robinson.

Nevertheless, his praise for *Spoon River Anthology* was lavish: 'perhaps the most original piece of literature that has been produced in America for a long time'. And he was dead right in calling it 'a novel in verse'. Masters, making his way as a lawyer for twenty years in the big city of Chicago, had been drawn back to memories of the small towns he grew up in, partly by a visit from his mother who must have filled his ears with local history and gossip. He had been aiming to write a novel out of this material when William Reedy, editor of *Reedy's Mirror*, a new literary and critical weekly in St. Louis, introduced him to Mackail's *Epigrams from the Greek Anthology* in the spring of 1914. Form and substance clicked together and Masters was off to the races. Saturated with nostalgia for a pastoral 'Old America' that he imagined existing in his grandparents' time and stirring with indignation at all that had gone wrong in the country and in himself, he tossed off over two hundred epitaphs within the year (after which he collapsed with pneumonia and nearly died). Reedy released these in weekly bunches, and Macmillan published the book in the following April in 1915. Within another year *Spoon River Anthology* had gone through nineteen printings, when a second edition added more poems (not included in the present volume since these detract more than they add to the total effect).

Braithwaite declared that *Spoon River* 'comes out of the West to meet Mr Frost's achievement in the East', a comparison that must have enraged both poets. In 1915 Frost, who has been castigated for his jealousies, called Masters his 'hated rival', but he was less intemperate than Masters, who boasted hubristically that Robinson and Frost 'were winnowing their gills for water high and dry on the sand bank until the *Spoon River* flood refreshed them with oxygen and enabled them to swim back into the stream'. And Frost was incisively perceptive in his unorthodox opinion that Masters 'was too romantic for my taste, and by romantic I'm afraid I mean among other things false-realistic'. The shock of the new that most readers felt from Masters' book was usually likened to the nitty-gritty 'naturalism' which novelists like Theodore Dreiser, a friend whom Masters sketched in 'Theodore the Poet', had dragged into American literature. Frost downplayed his criticism as 'but a qualification moreover of a real liking for the book. I like it better for what it is than for what a lot of people take it for.'

Whatever he meant by 'what it is', Frost was right in sensing an antirealistic, highly idealistic and 'romantic' counter-current to the main torrent of defeat and determinism sweeping Masters' characters to their dooms. A reader who starts at the beginning of the book and drives straight on might give up before reaching the strongest evidence of this amelioration. Reading from the back forward will give a more hopeful impression. Masters pointed out (hinting at an even greater hubris):

> 'When the book was put together in its definitive order, the fools, the drunkards, and the failures came first, the people of one-birth [*sic*] minds got second place, and the heroes and the enlightened spirits came last, a sort of *Divine Comedy*.'

Pride cometh before a fall, as both the Ancient Greeks and the 'Presbyterianism' he inveighed against should have warned him, and it is my impression that critics today consider almost all of Masters' voluminous works except *Spoon River* to be winnowing their gills high and dry on the sand bank, while Frost and Robinson are drinking deeply from the Castalian spring, much higher up Parnassus (a metaphor as cumbersome and needless as some of Masters').

On the other hand, the spawn of *Spoon River* can be spotted everywhere. When a new novel 'explores the intertwined fates of marginal, small-town people' scarred in body and mind, willy-nilly we are in Masters country. When a poet 'longs for his own paradise lost, the joy and the place of his childhood', he is swimming back to the source from which Masters drew his great inspiration. Even in the forms of their cadenced, free verse, mostly end-stopped lines, twenty or so at a time, sketching a portrait or character study as in silhouette, the poets of America's little magazines are paying their tribute to these poems which they read first in school and maybe spent their babysitting money on. Warts and all, this is a toad that hasn't swum away.

– John Ridland, 2005

Bibliographical Note:

Masters' biography is written comprehensively and respectfully by Herbert K. Russell (University of Illinois Press, 2001). The endnotes to the present edition have benefited from John E. Hallwas' scholarship in *Spoon River Anthology: An Annotated Edition* (University of Illinois Press, 1991).

Note on the Text:

The present edition follows the 1915 first edition of the book, with some modernisation of Masters' dated and sometimes careless punctuation.

Spoon River Anthology

The Hill

Where are Elmer, Herman, Bert, Tom and Charley,
The weak of will, the strong of arm, the clown, the boozer, the fighter?
All, all are sleeping on the hill.

One passed in a fever,
One was burned in a mine,
One was killed in a brawl,
One died in a jail,
One fell from a bridge toiling for children and wife –
All, all are sleeping, sleeping, sleeping on the hill.

Where are Ella, Kate, Mag, Lizzie and Edith,   10
The tender heart, the simple soul, the loud, the proud, the happy one? –
All, all are sleeping on the hill.

One died in shameful childbirth,
One of a thwarted love,
One at the hands of a brute in a brothel,
One of a broken pride, in the search for heart's desire;
One after life in far-away London and Paris
Was brought to her little space by Ella and Kate and Mag –
All, all are sleeping, sleeping, sleeping on the hill.

Where are Uncle Isaac and Aunt Emily,   20
And old Towny Kincaid and Sevigne Houghton,
And Major Walker who had talked
With venerable men of the revolution? –
All, all are sleeping on the hill.

They brought them dead sons from the war,
And daughters whom life had crushed,
And their children fatherless, crying –
All, all are sleeping, sleeping, sleeping on the hill.

Where is Old Fiddler Jones
Who played with life all his ninety years,
Braving the sleet with bared breast,
Drinking, rioting, thinking neither of wife nor kin,
Nor gold, nor love, nor heaven?
Lo! he babbles of the fish-fries of long ago,
Of the horse-races of long ago at Clary's Grove,
Of what Abe Lincoln said
One time at Springfield.

Hod Putt

Here I lie close to the grave
Of Old Bill Piersol,
Who grew rich trading with the Indians, and who
Afterwards took the Bankrupt Law
And emerged from it richer than ever.
Myself grown tired of toil and poverty
And beholding how Old Bill and others grew in wealth,
Robbed a traveler one Night near Proctor's Grove,
Killing him unwittingly while doing so,
For the which I was tried and hanged.   10
That was my way of going into bankruptcy.
Now we who took the bankrupt law in our respective ways
Sleep peacefully side by side.

Ollie McGee

Have you seen walking through the village
A man with downcast eyes and haggard face?
That is my husband who, by secret cruelty
Never to be told, robbed me of my youth and my beauty,
Till at last, wrinkled and with yellow teeth,
And with broken pride and shameful humility,
I sank into the grave.
But what think you gnaws at my husband's heart?
The face of what I was, the face of what he made me!
These are driving him to the place where I lie.   10
In death, therefore, I am avenged.

Fletcher McGee

She took my strength by minutes,
She took my life by hours,
She drained me like a fevered moon
That saps the spinning world.
The days went by like shadows,
The minutes wheeled like stars.
She took the pity from my heart
And made it into smiles.
She was a hunk of sculptor's clay,
My secret thoughts were fingers: 10
They flew behind her pensive brow
And lined it deep with pain.
They set the lips, and sagged the cheeks,
And drooped the eye with sorrow.
My soul had entered in the clay,
Fighting like seven devils.
It was not mine, it was not hers;
She held it, but its struggles
Modeled a face she hated,
And a face I feared to see.   20
I beat the windows, shook the bolts.
I hid me in a corner
And then she died and haunted me,
And hunted me for life.

Robert Fulton Tanner

If a man could bite the giant hand
That catches and destroys him,
As I was bitten by a rat
While demonstrating my patent trap,
In my hardware store that day.
But a man can never avenge himself
On the monstrous ogre Life.
You enter the room – that's being born;
And then you must live – work out your soul.
Aha! the bait that you crave is in view: 10
A woman with money you want to marry,
Prestige, place, or power in the world.
But there's work to do and things to conquer –
Oh, yes! the wires that screen the bait.
At last you get in – but you hear a step:
The ogre, Life, comes into the room,
(He was waiting and heard the clang of the spring)
To watch you nibble the wondrous cheese,
And stare with his burning eyes at you,
And scowl and laugh, and mock and curse you,   20
Running up and down in the trap,
Until your misery bores him.

Cassius Hueffer

They have chiseled on my stone the words:
'His life was gentle, and the elements so mixed in him
That nature might stand up and say to all the world,
This was a man.'
Those who knew me smile
As they read this empty rhetoric.

My epitaph should have been:
'Life was not gentle to him,
And the elements so mixed in him
That he made warfare on life   10
In the which he was slain.'
While I lived I could not cope with slanderous tongues,
Now that I am dead I must submit to an epitaph
Graven by a fool!

Serepta Mason

My life's blossom might have bloomed on all sides
Save for a bitter wind which stunted my petals
On the side of me which you in the village could see.
From the dust I lift a voice of protest:
My flowering side you never saw!
Ye living ones, ye are fools indeed
Who do not know the ways of the wind
And the unseen forces
That govern the processes of life.

Amanda Barker

Henry got me with child,
Knowing that I could not bring forth life
Without losing my own.
In my youth therefore I entered the portals of dust.
Traveler, it is believed in the village where I lived
That Henry loved me with a husband's love
But I proclaim from the dust
That he slew me to gratify his hatred.

Chase Henry

In life I was the town drunkard;
When I died the priest denied me burial
In holy ground.
The which redounded to my good fortune.
For the Protestants bought this lot,
And buried my body here,
Close to the grave of the banker Nicholas,
And of his wife Priscilla.
Take note, ye prudent and pious souls,
Of the cross-currents in life   10
Which bring honor to the dead, who lived in shame

Judge Somers

How does it happen, tell me,
That I who was most erudite of lawyers,
Who knew Blackstone and Coke
Almost by heart, who made the greatest speech
The courthouse ever heard, and wrote
A brief that won the praise of Justice Breese –
How does it happen, tell me,
That I lie here unmarked, forgotten,
While Chase Henry, the town drunkard,
Has a marble block, topped by an urn,   10
Wherein Nature, in a mood ironical,
Has sown a flowering weed?

Benjamin Pantier

Together in this grave lie Benjamin Pantier, attorney at law,
And Nig, his dog, constant companion, solace and friend.
Down the gray road, friends, children, men and women,
Passing one by one out of life, left me till I was alone
With Nig for partner, bed-fellow; comrade in drink.
In the morning of life I knew aspiration and saw glory,
Then she, who survives me, snared my soul
With a snare which bled me to death,
Till I, once strong of will, lay broken, indifferent,
Living with Nig in a room back of a dingy office.   10
Under my jaw-bone is snuggled the bony nose of Nig –
Our story is lost in silence. Go by, mad world!

Mrs Benjamin Pantier

I know that he told that I snared his soul
With a snare which bled him to death.
And all the men loved him,
And most of the women pitied him.
But suppose you are really a lady, and have delicate tastes,
And loathe the smell of whiskey and onions,
And the rhythm of Wordsworth's 'Ode' runs in your ears,
While he goes about from morning till night
Repeating bits of that common thing,
'Oh, why should the spirit of mortal be proud?'   10
And then, suppose;
You are a woman well endowed,
And the only man with whom the law and morality
Permit you to have the marital relation
Is the very man that fills you with disgust
Every time you think of it – while you think of it
Every time you see him?
That's why I drove him away from home
To live with his dog in a dingy room
Back of his office.   20

Reuben Pantier

Well, Emily Sparks, your prayers were not wasted,
Your love was not all in vain.
I owe whatever I was in life
To your hope that would not give me up,
To your love that saw me still as good.
Dear Emily Sparks, let me tell you the story.
I pass the effect of my father and mother;
The milliner's daughter made me trouble
And out I went in the world,
Where I passed through every peril known   10
Of wine and women and joy of life.
One night, in a room in the Rue de Rivoli,
I was drinking wine with a black-eyed cocotte,
And the tears swam into my eyes.
She though they were amorous tears and smiled
For thought of her conquest over me.
But my soul was three thousand miles away,
In the days when you taught me in Spoon River.
And just because you no more could love me,
Nor pray for me, nor write me letters,   20
The eternal silence of you spoke instead.
And the black-eyed cocotte took the tears for hers,
As well as the deceiving kisses I gave her.
Somehow, from that hour, I had a new vision –
Dear Emily Sparks!

Emily Sparks

Where is my boy, my boy –
In what far part of the world?
The boy I loved best of all in the school? –
I, the teacher, the old maid, the virgin heart,
Who made them all my children.
Did I know my boy aright,
Thinking of him as a spirit aflame,
Active, ever aspiring?
Oh, boy, boy, for whom I prayed and prayed
In many a watchful hour at night,   10
Do you remember the letter I wrote you
Of the beautiful love of Christ?
And whether you ever took it or not,
My boy, wherever you are,
Work for your soul's sake,
That all the clay of you, all the dross of you,
May yield to the fire of you,
Till the fire is nothing but light!…
Nothing but light!

Trainor, the Druggist

Only the chemist can tell, and not always the chemist,
What will result from compounding
Fluids or solids.
And who can tell
How men and women will interact
On each other, or what children will result?
There were Benjamin Pantier and his wife,
Good in themselves, but evil toward each other:
He oxygen, she hydrogen,
Their son, a devastating fire.   10
I, Trainor, the druggist, a mixer of chemicals,
Killed while making an experiment,
Lived unwedded.

Daisy Fraser

Did you ever hear of Editor Whedon
Giving to the public treasury any of the money he received
For supporting candidates for office?
Or for writing up the canning factory
To get people to invest?
Or for suppressing the facts about the bank,
When it was rotten and ready to break?
Did you ever hear of the Circuit Judge
Helping anyone except the 'Q' railroad,
Or the bankers? Or did Revd Peet or Revd Sibley   10
Give any part of their salary, earned by keeping still,
Or speaking out as the leaders wished them to do,
To the building of the water works?
But I, Daisy Fraser, who always passed
Along the streets through rows of nods and smiles,
And coughs and words such as 'there she goes,'
Never was taken before Justice Arnett
Without contributing ten dollars and costs
To the school fund of Spoon River!

Their spirits beat upon mine
Like the wings of a thousand butterflies.
I closed my eyes and felt their spirits vibrating.
I closed my eyes, yet I knew when their lashes
Fringed their cheeks from downcast eyes,
And when they turned their heads,
And when their garments clung to them,
Or fell from them, in exquisite draperies.
Their spirits watched my ecstasy
With wide looks of starry unconcern.   10
Their spirits looked upon my torture;
They drank it as it were the water of life,
With reddened cheeks, brightened eyes,
The rising flame of my soul made their spirits gilt,
Like the wings of a butterfly drifting suddenly into sunlight.
And they cried to me for life, life, life.
But in taking life for myself,
In seizing and crushing their souls,
As a child crushes grapes and drinks
From its palms the purple juice,   20
I came to this wingless void,
Where neither red, nor gold, nor wine,
Nor the rhythm of life is known.

Minerva Jones

I am Minerva, the village poetess,
Hooted at, jeered at by the Yahoos of the street
For my heavy body, cock-eye, and rolling walk,
And all the more when 'Butch' Weldy
Captured me after a brutal hunt.
He left me to my fate with Dr Meyers,
And I sank into death, growing numb from the feet up,
Like one stepping deeper and deeper into a stream of ice.
Will someone go to the village newspaper
And gather into a book the verses I wrote? –   10
I thirsted so for love!
I hungered so for life!

You would not believe, would you
That I came from good Welsh stock?
That I was purer-blooded than the white trash here?
And of more direct lineage than the New Englanders
And Virginians of Spoon River?
You would not believe that I had been to school
And read some books.
You saw me only as a run-down man
With matted hair and beard
And ragged clothes.   10
Sometimes a man's life turns into a cancer
From being bruised and continually bruised,
And swells into a purplish mass
Like growths on stalks of corn.
Here was I, a carpenter, mired in a bog of life
Into which I walked, thinking it was a meadow,
With a slattern for a wife, and poor Minerva, my daughter,
Whom you tormented and drove to death.
So I crept, crept, like a snail through the days
Of my life.   20
No more you hear my footsteps in the morning,
Resounding on the hollow sidewalk
Going to the grocery store for a little corn meal
And a nickel's-worth of bacon.

'Butch' Weldy

After I got religion and steadied down
They gave me a job in the canning works,
And every morning I had to fill
The tank in the yard with gasoline,
That fed the blow-fires in the sheds
To heat the soldering irons.
And I mounted a rickety ladder to do it,
Carrying buckets full of the stuff.
One morning, as I stood there pouring,
The air grew still and seemed to heave,   10
And I shot up as the tank exploded,
And down I came with both legs broken,
And my eyes burned crisp as a couple of eggs.
For someone left a blow-fire going,
And something sucked the flame in the tank.
The Circuit Judge said whoever did it
Was a fellow-servant of mine, and so
Old Rhodes' son didn't have to pay me.
And I sat on the witness stand as blind
As Jack the Fiddler, saying over and over,   20
'I didn't know him at all.'

Dr Meyers

No other man, unless it was Doc Hill,
Did more for people in this town than I.
And all the weak, the halt, the improvident
And those who could not pay flocked to me.
I was good-hearted, easy Dr Meyers.
I was healthy, happy, in comfortable fortune,
Blest with a congenial mate, my children raised,
All wedded, doing well in the world.
And then one night, Minerva, the poetess,
Came to me in her trouble, crying.   10
I tried to help her out – she died –
They indicted me, the newspapers disgraced me,
My wife perished of a broken heart,
And pneumonia finished me.

Mrs Meyers

He protested all his life long
The newspapers lied about him villainously,
That he was not at fault for Minerva's fall,
But only tried to help her.
Poor soul so sunk in sin he could not see
That even trying to help her, as he called it,
He had broken the law human and divine.
Passers-by, an ancient admonition to you:
If your ways would be ways of pleasantness,
And all your pathways peace,   10
Love God and keep his commandments.

Knowlt Hoheimer

I was the first fruits of the Battle of Missionary Ridge.
When I felt the bullet enter my heart
I wished I had stayed at home and gone to jail
For stealing the hogs of Curl Trenary,
Instead of running away and joining the army.
Rather a thousand times the county jail
Than to lie under this marble figure with wings,
And this granite pedestal
Bearing the words, '*Pro Patria*.'
What do they mean, anyway?   10

Lydia Puckett

Knowlt Hoheimer ran away to the war
The day before Curl Trenary
Swore out a warrant through Justice Arnett
For stealing hogs.
But that's not the reason he turned a soldier.
He caught me running with Lucius Atherton.
We quarreled and I told him never again
To cross my path.
Then he stole the hogs and went to the war –
Back of every soldier is a woman.   10

Frank Drummer

Out of a cell into this darkened space –
The end at twenty-five!
My tongue could not speak what stirred within me,
And the village thought me a fool.
Yet at the start there was a clear vision,
A high and urgent purpose in my soul
Which drove me on trying to memorize
The *Encyclopedia Britannica*!

Hare Drummer

Do the boys and girls still go to Siever's
For cider, after school, in late September?
Or gather hazelnuts among the thickets
On Aaron Hatfield's farm when the frosts begin?
For many times with the laughing girls and boys
Played I along the road and over the hills
When the sun was low and the air was cool,
Stopping to club the walnut tree
Standing leafless against a flaming west.
Now, the smell of the autumn smoke,   10
And the dropping acorns,
And the echoes about the vales
Bring dreams of life. They hover over me.
They question me:
Where are those laughing comrades?
How many are with me, how many
In the old orchards along the way to Siever's,
And in the woods that overlook
The quiet water?

Doc Hill

I went up and down the streets
Here and there by day and night,
Through all hours of the night caring for the poor who were sick.
Do you know why?
My wife hated me, my son went to the dogs.
And I turned to the people and poured out my love to them.
Sweet it was to see the crowds about the lawns on the day of my funeral,
And hear them murmur their love and sorrow.
But oh, dear God, my soul trembled, scarcely able
To hold to the railing of the new life   10
When I saw Em Stanton behind the oak tree
At the grave,
Hiding herself, and her grief!

Sarah Brown

Maurice, weep not, I am not here under this pine tree.
The balmy air of spring whispers through the sweet grass,
The stars sparkle, the whippoorwill calls,
But thou grievest, while my soul lies rapturous
In the blest Nirvana of eternal light!
Go to the good heart that is my husband,
Who broods upon what he calls our guilty love:
Tell him that my love for you, no less than my love for him
Wrought out my destiny – that through the flesh
I won spirit, and through spirit, peace.   10
There is no marriage in heaven,
But there is love.

Percy Bysshe Shelley

My father who owned the wagon-shop
And grew rich shoeing horses
Sent me to the University of Montreal.
I learned nothing and returned home,
Roaming the fields with Bert Kessler,
Hunting quail and snipe.
At Thompson's Lake the trigger of my gun
Caught in the side of the boat
And a great hole was shot through my heart.
Over me a fond father erected this marble shaft,   10
On which stands the figure of a woman
Carved by an Italian artist.
They say the ashes of my namesake
Were scattered near the pyramid of Caius Cestius
Somewhere near Rome.

Flossie Cabanis

From Bindle's opera house in the village
To Broadway is a great step.
But I tried to take it, my ambition fired
When sixteen years of age,
Seeing *East Lynne* played here in the village
By Ralph Barrett, the coming
Romantic actor, who enthralled my soul.
True, I trailed back home, a broken failure,
When Ralph disappeared in New York,
Leaving me alone in the city –   10
But life broke him also.
In all this place of silence
There are no kindred spirits.
How I wish Duse could stand amid the pathos
Of these quiet fields
And read these words.

Julia Miller

We quarreled that morning,
For he was sixty-five, and I was thirty,
And I was nervous and heavy with the child
Whose birth I dreaded.
I thought over the last letter written me
By that estranged young soul
Whose betrayal of me I had concealed
By marrying the old man.
Then I took morphine and sat down to read.
Across the blackness that came over my eyes   10
I see the flickering light of these words even now:
'And Jesus said unto him, Verily
I say unto thee, Today thou shalt
Be with me in paradise.'

Johnnie Sayre

Father, thou canst never know
The anguish that smote my heart
For my disobedience, the moment I felt
The remorseless wheel of the engine
Sink into the crying flesh of my leg.
As they carried me to the home of widow Morris
I could see the schoolhouse in the valley
To which I played truant to steal rides upon the trains.
I prayed to live until I could ask your forgiveness –
And then your tears, your broken words of comfort!   10
From the solace of that hour I have gained infinite happiness.
Thou wert wise to chisel for me:
'Taken from the evil to come.'

Charlie French

Did you ever find out
Which one of the O'Brien boys it was
Who snapped the toy pistol against my hand?
There when the flags were red and white
In the breeze and 'Bucky' Estil
Was firing the cannon brought to Spoon River
From Vicksburg by Captain Harris;
And the lemonade stands were running
And the band was playing,
To have it all spoiled   10
By a piece of a cap shot under the skin of my hand,
And the boys all crowding about me saying:
'You'll die of lockjaw, Charlie, sure.'
Oh, dear! oh, dear!
What chum of mine could have done it?

Zenas Witt

I was sixteen, and I had the most terrible dreams,
And specks before my eyes, and nervous weakness.
And I couldn't remember the books I read,
Like Frank Drummer who memorized page after page.
And my back was weak, and I worried and worried,
And I was embarrassed and stammered my lessons,
And when I stood up to recite I'd forget
Everything that I had studied.
Well, I saw Dr Weese's advertisement,
And there I read everything in print, 10
Just as if he had known me,
And about the dreams which I couldn't help.
So I knew I was marked for an early grave.
And I worried until I had a cough,
And then the dreams stopped.
And then I slept the sleep without dreams
Here on the hill by the river.

Theodore the Poet

As a boy, Theodore, you sat for long hours
On the shore of the turbid Spoon
With deep-set eye staring at the door of the crawfish's burrow,
Waiting for him to appear, pushing ahead,
First his waving antennae, like straws of hay,
And soon his body, colored like soapstone,
Gemmed with eyes of jet.
And you wondered in a trance of thought
What he knew, what he desired, and why he lived at all.
But later your vision watched for men and women   10
Hiding in burrows of fate amid great cities,
Looking for the souls of them to come out,
So that you could see
How they lived, and for what,
And why they kept crawling so busily
Along the sandy way where water fails
As the summer wanes.

The Town Marshal

The Prohibitionists made me Town Marshal
When the saloons were voted out,
Because when I was a drinking man,
Before I joined the church, I killed a Swede
At the sawmill near Maple Grove.
And they wanted a terrible man,
Grim, righteous, strong, courageous,
And a hater of saloons and drinkers,
To keep law and order in the village.
And they presented me with a loaded cane   10
With which I struck Jack McGuire
Before he drew the gun with which he killed me.
The Prohibitionists spent their money in vain
To hang him, for in a dream
I appeared to one of the twelve jurymen
And told him the whole secret story.
Fourteen years were enough for killing me.

They would have lynched me
Had I not been secretly hurried away
To the jail at Peoria.
And yet I was going peacefully home,
Carrying my jug, a little drunk,
When Logan, the marshal, halted me,
Called me a drunken hound and shook me
And, when I cursed him for it, struck me
With that prohibition loaded cane –
All this before I shot him.   10
They would have hanged me except for this:
My lawyer, Kinsey Keene, was helping to land
Old Thomas Rhodes for wrecking the bank,
And the judge was a friend of Rhodes
And wanted him to escape,
And Kinsey offered to quit on Rhodes
For fourteen years for me.
And the bargain was made. I served my time
And learned to read and write.

Jacob Goodpasture

When Fort Sumter fell and the war came
I cried out in bitterness of soul:
'O glorious republic now no more!'
When they buried my soldier son
To the call of trumpets and the sound of drums
My heart broke beneath the weight
Of eighty years, and I cried:
'Oh, son who died in a cause unjust!
In the strife of Freedom slain!'
And I crept here under the grass.   10
And now from the battlements of time, behold:
Thrice thirty million souls being bound together
In the love of larger truth,
Rapt in the expectation of the birth
Of a new Beauty,
Sprung from Brotherhood and Wisdom.
I with eyes of spirit see the Transfiguration
Before you see it.
But ye infinite brood of golden eagles nesting ever higher,
Wheeling ever higher, the sunlight wooing   20
Of lofty places of Thought,
Forgive the blindness of the departed owl.

Dorcas Gustine

I was not beloved of the villagers,
But all because I spoke my mind,
And met those who transgressed against me
With plain remonstrance, hiding nor nurturing
Nor secret griefs nor grudges.
That act of the Spartan boy is greatly praised,
Who hid the wolf under his cloak,
Letting it devour him, uncomplainingly.
It is braver, I think, to snatch the wolf forth
And fight him openly, even in the street,   10
Amid dust and howls of pain.
The tongue may be an unruly member –
But silence poisons the soul.
Berate me who will – I am content.

Nicholas Bindle

Were you not ashamed, fellow citizens,
When my estate was probated and everyone knew
How small a fortune I left? –
You who hounded me in life,
To give, give, give to the churches, to the poor,
To the village! – me who had already given much.
And think you not I did not know
That the pipe-organ, which I gave to the church,
Played its christening songs when Deacon Rhodes,
Who broke and all but ruined me,   10
Worshipped for the first time after his acquittal?

Harold Arnett

I leaned against the mantel, sick, sick,
Thinking of my failure, looking into the abysm,
Weak from the noonday heat.
A church bell sounded mournfully far away,
I heard the cry of a baby,
And the coughing of John Yarnell,
Bed-ridden, feverish, feverish, dying,
Then the violent voice of my wife:
'Watch out, the potatoes are burning!'
I smelled them... then there was irresistible disgust.   10
I pulled the trigger... blackness... light...
Unspeakable regret... fumbling for the world again.
Too late! Thus I came here,
With lungs for breathing... one cannot breathe here with lungs,
Though one must breathe... Of what use is it
To rid one's self of the world,
When no soul may ever escape the eternal destiny of life?

Margaret Fuller Slack

I would have been as great as George Eliot
But for an untoward fate.
For look at the photograph of me made by Penniwit,
Chin resting on hand, and deep-set eyes –
Gray, too, and far-searching.
But there was the old, old problem:
Should it be celibacy, matrimony or unchastity?
Then John Slack, the rich druggist, wooed me,
Luring me with the promise of leisure for my novel,
And I married him, giving birth to eight children,   10
And had no time to write.
It was all over with me, anyway,
When I ran the needle in my hand
While washing the baby's things,
And died from lockjaw, an ironical death.
Hear me, ambitious souls,
Sex is the curse of life!

George Trimble

Do you remember when I stood on the steps
Of the courthouse and talked free-silver,
And the single-tax of Henry George?
Then do you remember that, when the Peerless Leader
Lost the first battle, I began to talk prohibition,
And became active in the church?
That was due to my wife,
Who pictured to me my destruction
If I did not prove my morality to the people.
Well, she ruined me: 10
For the radicals grew suspicious of me,
And the conservatives were never sure of me –
And here I lie, unwept of all.

'Ace' Shaw

I never saw any difference
Between playing cards for money
And selling real estate,
Practicing law, banking, or anything else.
For everything is chance.
Nevertheless
Seest thou a man diligent in business?
He shall stand before Kings!

My wife lost her health,
And dwindled until she weighed scarce ninety pounds.
Then that woman, whom the men
Styled Cleopatra, came along.
And we – we married ones –
All broke our vows, myself among the rest.
Years passed and one by one
Death claimed them all in some hideous form
And I was borne along by dreams
Of God's particular grace for me,   10
And I began to write, write, write, reams on reams
Of the second coming of Christ.
Then Christ came to me and said,
'Go into the church and stand before the congregation
And confess your sin.'
But just as I stood up and began to speak
I saw my little girl, who was sitting in the front seat –
My little girl who was born blind!
After that, all is blackness.

Aner Clute

Over and over they used to ask me,
While buying the wine or the beer,
In Peoria first, and later in Chicago,
Denver, Frisco, New York, wherever I lived,
How I happened to lead the life,
And what was the start of it.
Well, I told them a silk dress,
And a promise of marriage from a rich man –
(It was Lucius Atherton).
But that was not really it at all.   10
Suppose a boy steals an apple
From the tray at the grocery store,
And they all begin to call him a thief,
The editor, minister, judge, and all the people –
'A thief', 'a thief', 'a thief', wherever he goes.
And he can't get work, and he can't get bread
Without stealing it, why the boy will steal.
It's the way the people regard the theft of the apple
That makes the boy what he is.

Lucius Atherton

When my moustache curled,
And my hair was black,
And I wore tight trousers
And a diamond stud,
I was an excellent knave of hearts and took many a trick.
But when the gray hairs began to appear –
Lo! a new generation of girls
Laughed at me, not fearing me,
And I had no more exciting adventures
Wherein I was all but shot for a heartless devil,   10
But only drabby affairs, warmed-over affairs
Of other days and other men.
And time went on until I lived at Mayer's restaurant,
Partaking of short-orders, a gray, untidy,
Toothless, discarded, rural Don Juan…
There is a mighty shade here who sings
Of one named Beatrice,
And I see now that the force that made him great
Drove me to the dregs of life.

Homer Clapp

Often Aner Clute at the gate
Refused me the parting kiss,
Saying we should be engaged before that,
And just with a distant clasp of the hand
She bade me good night, as I brought her home
From the skating rink or the revival.
No sooner did my departing footsteps die away
Than Lucius Atherton,
(So I learned when Aner went to Peoria)
Stole in at her window, or took her riding   10
Behind his spanking team of bays
Into the country.
The shock of it made me settle down
And I put all the money I got from my father's estate
Into the canning factory, to get the job
Of head accountant, and lost it all.
And then I knew I was one of Life's fools,
Whom only Death would treat as the equal
Of other men, making me feel like a man.

Deacon Taylor

I belonged to the church,
And to the party of prohibition,
And the villagers thought I died of eating watermelon.
In truth I had cirrhosis of the liver,
For every noon for thirty years,
I slipped behind the prescription partition
In Trainor's drug store
And poured a generous drink
From the bottle marked '*Spiritus frumenti.*'

Sam Hookey

I ran away from home with the circus,
Having fallen in love with Mademoiselle Estralada,
The lion tamer.
One time, having starved the lions
For more than a day,
I entered the cage and began to beat Brutus
And Leo and Gypsy.
Whereupon Brutus sprang upon me,
And killed me.
On entering these regions   10
I met a shadow who cursed me,
And said it served me right…
It was Robespierre!

I inherited forty acres from my Father
And, by working my wife, my two sons and two daughters
From dawn to dusk, I acquired
A thousand acres. But not content,
Wishing to own two thousand acres,
I bustled through the years with axe and plow,
Toiling, denying myself, my wife, my sons, my daughters.
Squire Higbee wrongs me to say
That I died from smoking Red Eagle cigars.
Eating hot pie and gulping coffee   10
During the scorching hours of harvest-time
Brought me here ere I had reached my sixtieth year.

Fiddler Jones

The earth keeps some vibration going
There in your heart, and that is you.
And if the people find you can fiddle,
Why, fiddle you must, for all your life.
What do you see, a harvest of clover?
Or a meadow to walk through to the river?
The wind's in the corn, you rub your hands
For beeves hereafter ready for market,
Or else you hear the rustle of skirts
Like the girls when dancing at Little Grove.   10
To Cooney Potter a pillar of dust
Or whirling leaves meant ruinous drouth.
They looked to me like Red-Head Sammy
Stepping it off, to 'Toor-a-Loor'.
How could I till my forty acres,
Not to speak of getting more,
With a medley of horns, bassoons and piccolos
Stirred in my brain by crows and robins
And the creak of a windmill – only these?
And I never started to plow in my life   20
That someone did not stop in the road
And take me away to a dance or picnic.
I ended up with forty acres.
I ended up with a broken fiddle –
And a broken laugh, and a thousand memories,
And not a single regret.

I was only eight years old,
And before I grew up and knew what it meant
I had no words for it, except
That I was frightened and told my Mother,
And that my Father got a pistol
And would have killed Charlie, who was a big boy,
Fifteen years old, except for his Mother.
Nevertheless the story clung to me.
But the man who married me, a widower of thirty-five,
Was a newcomer and never heard it   10
'Till two years after we were married.
Then he considered himself cheated,
And the village agreed that I was not really a virgin.
Well, he deserted me, and I died
The following winter.

Louise Smith

Herbert broke our engagement of eight years
When Annabelle returned to the village
From the Seminary. Ah me!
If I had let my love for him alone
It might have grown into a beautiful sorrow –
Who knows? – filling my life with healing fragrance.
But I tortured it, I poisoned it,
I blinded its eyes, and it became hatred –
Deadly ivy instead of clematis.
And my soul fell from its support,   10
Its tendrils tangled in decay.
Do not let the will play gardener to your soul
Unless you are sure
It is wiser than your soul's nature.

All your sorrow, Louise, and hatred of me
Sprang from your delusion that it was wantonness
Of spirit and contempt of your soul's rights
Which made me turn to Annabelle and forsake you.
You really grew to hate me for love of me,
Because I was your soul's happiness,
Formed and tempered
To solve your life for you, and would not.
But you were my misery. If you had been
My happiness would I not have clung to you?   10
This is life's sorrow:
That one can be happy only where two are,
And that our hearts are drawn to stars
Which want us not.

George Gray

I have studied many times
The marble which was chiseled for me –
A boat with a furled sail at rest in a harbor.
In truth it pictures not my destination
But my life.
For love was offered me and I shrank from its disillusionment;
Sorrow knocked at my door, but I was afraid;
Ambition called to me, but I dreaded the chances.
Yet all the while I hungered for meaning in my life.
And now I know that we must lift the sail   10
And catch the winds of destiny
Wherever they drive the boat.
To put meaning in one's life may end in madness,
But life without meaning is the torture
Of restlessness and vague desire –
It is a boat longing for the sea and yet afraid.

It never came into my mind
Until I was ready to die
That Jenny had loved me to death, with malice of heart.
For I was seventy, she was thirty-five,
And I wore myself to a shadow trying to husband
Jenny, rosy Jenny full of the ardor of life.
For all my wisdom and grace of mind
Gave her no delight at all, in very truth,
But ever and anon she spoke of the giant strength
Of Willard Shafer, and of his wonderful feat   10
Of lifting a traction engine out of the ditch
One time at Georgie Kirby's.
So Jenny inherited my fortune and married Willard –
That mount of brawn! That clownish soul!

Griffy the Cooper

The cooper should know about tubs.
But I learned about life as well,
And you who loiter around these graves
Think you know life.
You think your eye sweeps about a wide horizon, perhaps:
In truth you are only looking around the interior of your tub.
You cannot lift yourself to its rim
And see the outer world of things,
And at the same time see yourself.
You are submerged in the tub of yourself –   10
Taboos and rules and appearances
Are the staves of your tub.
Break them and dispel the witchcraft
Of thinking your tub is life!
And that you know life!

A.D. Blood

If you in the village think that my work was a good one,
Who closed the saloons and stopped all playing at cards,
And haled old Daisy Fraser before Justice Arnett,
In many a crusade to purge the people of sin,
Why do you let the milliner's daughter Dora,
And the worthless son of Benjamin Pantier
Nightly make my grave their unholy pillow?

Dora Williams

When Reuben Pantier ran away and threw me
I went to Springfield. There I met a lush,
Whose father, just deceased, left him a fortune.
He married me when drunk. My life was wretched.
A year passed and one day they found him dead.
That made me rich. I moved on to Chicago.
After a time met Tyler Rountree, villain.
I moved on to New York. A gray-haired magnate
Went mad about me – so another fortune.
He died one night right in my arms, you know.   10
(I saw his purple face for years thereafter.)
There was almost a scandal. I moved on,
This time to Paris. I was now a woman,
Insidious, subtle, versed in the world and rich.
My sweet apartment near the Champs Elysées
Became a center for all sorts of people,
Musicians, poets, dandies, artists, nobles,
Where we spoke French and German, Italian, English.
I wed Count Navigato, native of Genoa.
We went to Rome. He poisoned me, I think.   20
Now in the Campo Santo overlooking
The sea where young Columbus dreamed new worlds,
See what they chiseled: '*Contessa Navigato*
Implora eterna quiete.'

I was the milliner
Talked about, lied about,
Mother of Dora,
Whose strange disappearance
Was charged to her rearing.
My eye quick to beauty
Saw much beside ribbons
And buckles and feathers
And leghorns and felts,
To set off sweet faces,   10
And dark hair and gold.
One thing I will tell you
And one I will ask:
The stealers of husbands
Wear powder and trinkets,
And fashionable hats.
Wives, wear them yourselves.
Hats may make divorces –
They also prevent them.
Well now, let me ask you: 20
If all of the children, born here in Spoon River
Had been reared by the County, somewhere on a farm,
And the fathers and mothers had been given their freedom
To live and enjoy, change mates if they wished,
Do you think that Spoon River
Had been any the worse?

William and Emily

There is something about
Death like love itself!
If with someone with whom you have known passion,
And the glow of youthful love,
You also, after years of life
Together, feel the sinking of the fire
And thus fade away together,
Gradually, faintly, delicately,
As it were in each other's arms,
Passing from the familiar room –   10
That is a power of unison between souls
Like love itself!

Take note, passers-by, of the sharp erosions
Eaten in my headstone by the wind and rain –
Almost as if an intangible Nemesis or hatred
Were marking scores against me,
But to destroy, and not preserve, my memory.
I in life was the Circuit Judge, a maker of notches,
Deciding cases on the points the lawyers scored,
Not on the right of the matter.
O wind and rain, leave my headstone alone!
For worse than the anger of the wronged,   10
The curses of the poor,
Was to lie speechless, yet with vision clear,
Seeing that even Hod Putt, the murderer,
Hanged by my sentence,
Was innocent in soul compared with me.

Blind Jack

I had fiddled all day at the county fair.
But driving home 'Butch' Weldy and Jack McGuire,
Who were roaring full, made me fiddle and fiddle
To the song of 'Susie Skinner', while whipping the horses
Till they ran away.
Blind as I was, I tried to get out
As the carriage fell in the ditch,
And was caught in the wheels and killed.
There's a blind man here with a brow
As big and white as a cloud.   10
And all we fiddlers, from highest to lowest,
Writers of music and tellers of stories,
Sit at his feet,
And hear him sing of the fall of Troy.

I won the prize essay at school
Here in the village,
And published a novel before I was twenty-five.
I went to the city for themes and to enrich my art,
There married the banker's daughter,
And later became president of the bank –
Always looking forward to some leisure
To write an epic novel of the war.
Meanwhile friend of the great, and lover of letters,
And host to Matthew Arnold and to Emerson.   10
An after-dinner speaker, writing essays
For local clubs. At last brought here –
My boyhood home, you know –
Not even a little tablet in Chicago
To keep my name alive.
How great it is to write the single line:
'Roll on, thou deep and dark blue Ocean, roll!'[1]

Nancy Knapp

Well, don't you see this was the way of it:
We bought the farm with what he inherited,
And his brothers and sisters accused him of poisoning
His father's mind against the rest of them.
And we never had any peace with our treasure.
The murrain took the cattle, and the crops failed.
And lightning struck the granary.
So we mortgaged the farm to keep going.
And he grew silent and was worried all the time.
Then some of the neighbors refused to speak to us,   10
And took sides with his brothers and sisters.
And I had no place to turn, as one may say to himself,
At an earlier time in life, 'No matter,
So and so is my friend, or I can shake this off
With a little trip to Decatur.'
Then the dreadfulest smells infested the rooms.
So I set fire to the beds and the old witch-house
Went up in a roar of flame,
As I danced in the yard with waving arms,
While he wept like a freezing steer.   20

The very fall my sister Nancy Knapp
Set fire to the house
They were trying Dr Duval
For the murder of Zora Clemens,
And I sat in the court two weeks
Listening to every witness.
It was clear he had got her in a family way,
And to let the child be born
Would not do.
Well, how about me with eight children,   10
And one coming, and the farm
Mortgaged to Thomas Rhodes?
And when I got home that night,
(After listening to the story of the buggy ride,
And the finding of Zora in the ditch,)
The first thing I saw, right there by the steps,
Where the boys had hacked for angleworms,
Was the hatchet!
And just as I entered there was my wife,
Standing before me, big with child.   20
She started the talk of the mortgaged farm,
And I killed her.

I, the scourge-wielder, balance-wrecker,
Smiter with whips and swords;
I, hater of the breakers of the law;
I, legalist, inexorable and bitter,
Driving the jury to hang the madman, Barry Holden,
Was made as one dead by light too bright for eyes,
And woke to face a Truth with bloody brow:
Steel forceps fumbled by a doctor's hand
Against my boy's head as he entered life
Made him an idiot.   10
I turned to books of science[2]
To care for him.
That's how the world of those whose minds are sick
Became my work in life, and all my world.
Poor ruined boy! You were, at last, the potter
And I and all my deeds of charity
The vessels of your hand.

Wendell P. Bloyd

They first charged me with disorderly conduct,
There being no statute on blasphemy.
Later they locked me up as insane
Where I was beaten to death by a Catholic guard.
My offense was this:
I said God lied to Adam, and destined him
To lead the life of a fool,
Ignorant that there is evil in the world as well as good.
And when Adam outwitted God by eating the apple
And saw through the lie,   10
God drove him out of Eden to keep him from taking
The fruit of immortal life.
For Christ's sake, you sensible people,
Here's what God Himself says about it in the book of Genesis:
'And the Lord God said, behold the man
Is become as one of us' (a little envy, you see),
'To know good and evil' (the all-is-good lie exposed):
'And now lest he put forth his hand and take
Also of the tree of life and eat, and live forever:
Therefore the Lord God sent him forth from the garden of Eden.'   20
(The reason I believe God crucified His Own Son
To get out of the wretched tangle is, because it sounds just like Him.)

Francis Turner

I could not run or play
In boyhood.
In manhood I could only sip the cup,
Not drink –
For scarlet-fever left my heart diseased.
Yet I lie here
Soothed by a secret none but Mary knows:
There is a garden of acacia,
Catalpa trees, and arbors sweet with vines –
There on that afternoon in June   10
By Mary's side –
Kissing her with my soul upon my lips
It suddenly took flight.

Franklin Jones

If I could have lived another year
I could have finished my flying machine,
And become rich and famous.
Hence it is fitting the workman
Who tried to chisel a dove for me
Made it look more like a chicken.
For what is it all but being hatched,
And running about the yard,
To the day of the block?
Save that a man has an angel's brain,   10
And sees the axe from the first!

John M. Church

I was attorney for the 'Q'
And the Indemnity Company which insured
The owners of the mine.
I pulled the wires with judge and jury,
And the upper courts, to beat the claims
Of the crippled, the widow and orphan,
And made a fortune thereat.
The bar association sang my praises
In a high-flown resolution.
And the floral tributes were many –   10
But the rats devoured my heart
And a snake made a nest in my skull.

I, born in Weimar
Of a mother who was French
And German father, a most learned professor,
Orphaned at fourteen years,
Became a dancer, known as Russian Sonia,
All up and down the boulevards of Paris,
Mistress betimes of sundry dukes and counts,
And later of poor artists and of poets.
At forty years, *passée*, I sought New York
And met old Patrick Hummer on the boat,   10
Red-faced and hale, though turned his sixtieth year,
Returning after having sold a ship-load
Of cattle in the German city, Hamburg.
He brought me to Spoon River and we lived here
For twenty years – they thought that we were married!
This oak tree near me is the favorite haunt
Of blue jays chattering, chattering all the day.
And why not? for my very dust is laughing
For thinking of the humorous thing called life.

Barney Hainsfeather

If the excursion train to Peoria
Had just been wrecked, I might have escaped with my life –
Certainly I should have escaped this place.
But as it was burned as well, they mistook me
For John Allen who was sent to the Hebrew Cemetery
At Chicago,
And John for me, so I lie here.
It was bad enough to run a clothing store in this town,
But to be buried here – *ach!*

Seeds in a dry pod, tick, tick, tick,
Tick, tick, tick, like mites in a quarrel –
Faint iambics that the full breeze wakens –
But the pine tree makes a symphony thereof.
Triolets, villanelles, rondels, rondeaus,
Ballades by the score with the same old thought:
The snows and the roses of yesterday are vanished,
And what is love but a rose that fades?
Life all around me here in the village:
Tragedy, comedy, valor and truth,   10
Courage, constancy, heroism, failure –
All in the loom, and oh what patterns!
Woodlands, meadows, streams and rivers –
Blind to all of it all my life long.
Triolets, villanelles, rondels, rondeaus,
Seeds in a dry pod, tick, tick, tick,
Tick, tick, tick, what little iambics,
While Homer and Whitman roared in the pines?

Pauline Barrett

Almost the shell of a woman after the surgeon's knife!
And almost a year to creep back into strength,
Till the dawn of our wedding decennial
Found me my seeming self again.
We walked the forest together,
By a path of soundless moss and turf.
But I could not look in your eyes,
And you could not look in my eyes,
For such sorrow was ours – the beginning of gray in your hair,
And I but a shell of myself.   10
And what did we talk of? – sky and water,
Anything, 'most, to hide our thoughts.
And then your gift of wild roses,
Set on the table to grace our dinner.
Poor heart, how bravely you struggled
To imagine and live a remembered rapture!
Then my spirit drooped as the night came on,
And you left me alone in my room for a while,
As you did when I was a bride, poor heart.
And I looked in the mirror and something said: 20
'One should be all dead when one is half-dead –
Nor ever mock life, nor ever cheat love.'
And I did it looking there in the mirror –
Dear, have you ever understood?

Reverend Wiley advised me not to divorce him
For the sake of the children,
And Judge Somers advised him the same.
So we stuck to the end of the path.
But two of the children thought he was right,
And two of the children thought I was right.
And the two who sided with him blamed me,
And the two who sided with me blamed him,
And they grieved for the one they sided with.
And all were torn with the guilt of judging,   10
And tortured in soul because they could not admire
Equally him and me.
Now every gardener knows that plants grown in cellars
Or under stones are twisted and yellow and weak.
And no mother would let her baby suck
Diseased milk from her breast.
Yet preachers and judges advise the raising of souls
Where there is no sunlight, but only twilight,
No warmth, but only dampness and cold –
Preachers and judges!   20

Mrs George Reece

To this generation I would say:
Memorize some bit of verse of truth or beauty.
It may serve a turn in your life.
My husband had nothing to do
With the fall of the bank – he was only cashier.
The wreck was due to the president, Thomas Rhodes,
And his vain, unscrupulous son.
Yet my husband was sent to prison,
And I was left with the children,
To feed and clothe and school them.   10
And I did it, and sent them forth
Into the world all clean and strong,
And all through the wisdom of Pope, the poet:
'Act well your part, there all the honor lies.'

I preached four thousand sermons,
I conducted forty revivals,
And baptized many converts.
Yet no deed of mine
Shines brighter in the memory of the world,
And none is treasured more by me:
Look how I saved the Blisses from divorce,
And kept the children free from that disgrace,
To grow up into moral men and women,
Happy themselves, a credit to the village.   10

Thomas Ross, Jr

This I saw with my own eyes:
A cliff – swallow
Made her nest in a hole of the high clay-bank
There near Miller's Ford.
But no sooner were the young hatched
Than a snake crawled up to the nest
To devour the brood.
Then the mother swallow with swift flutterings
And shrill cries
Fought at the snake, 10
Blinding him with the beat of her wings,
Until he, wriggling and rearing his head,
Fell backward down the bank
Into Spoon River and was drowned.
Scarcely an hour passed
Until a shrike
Impaled the mother swallow on a thorn.
As for myself I overcame my lower nature
Only to be destroyed by my brother's ambition.

I had no objection at all
To selling my household effects at auction
On the village square.
It gave my beloved flock the chance
To get something which had belonged to me
For a memorial.
But that trunk which was struck off
To Burchard, the grog-keeper!
Did you know it contained the manuscripts
Of a lifetime of sermons?   10
And he burned them as waste paper.

My valiant fight! For I call it valiant,
With my father's beliefs from old Virginia:
Hating slavery, but no less war.
I, full of spirit, audacity, courage,
Thrown into life here in Spoon River,
With its dominant forces drawn from New England,
Republicans, Calvinists, merchants, bankers,
Hating me, yet fearing my arm.
With wife and children heavy to carry –
Yet fruits of my very zest of life.   10
Stealing odd pleasures that cost me prestige,
And reaping evils I had not sown;
Foe of the church with its charnel dankness,
Friend of the human touch of the tavern;
Tangled with fates all alien to me,
Deserted by hands I called my own.
Then just as I felt my giant strength
Short of breath, behold my children
Had wound their lives in stranger gardens –
And I stood alone, as I started alone!   20
My valiant life! I died on my feet,
Facing the silence – facing the prospect
That no one would know of the fight I made.

Albert Schirding

Jonas Keene thought his lot a hard one
Because his children were all failures.
But I know of a fate more trying than that:
It is to be a failure while your children are successes.
For I raised a brood of eagles
Who flew away at last, leaving me
A crow on the abandoned bough.
Then, with the ambition to prefix Honorable to my name,
And thus to win my children's admiration,
I ran for County Superintendent of Schools,   10
Spending my accumulations to win – and lost.
That fall my daughter received first prize in Paris
For her picture, entitled, 'The Old Mill' –
(It was of the water mill before Henry Wilkin put in steam.)
The feeling that I was not worthy of her finished me.

Jonas Keene

Why did Albert Schirding kill himself
Trying to be County Superintendent of Schools,
Blest as he was with the means of life
And wonderful children, bringing him honor
Ere he was sixty?
If even one of my boys could have run a news-stand,
Or one of my girls could have married a decent man,
I should not have walked in the rain
And jumped into bed with clothes all wet,
Refusing medical aid.   10

Yee Bow

They got me into the Sunday School
In Spoon River
And tried to get me to drop Confucius for Jesus.
I could have been no worse off
If I had tried to get them to drop Jesus for Confucius.
For, without any warning, as if it were a prank,
And sneaking up behind me, Harry Wiley,
The minister's son, caved my ribs into my lungs,
With a blow of his fist.
Now I shall never sleep with my ancestors in Peking,   10
And no children shall worship at my grave.

Washington McNeely

Rich, honored by my fellow citizens,
The father of many children, born of a noble mother,
All raised there
In the great mansion-house, at the edge of town.
Note the cedar tree on the lawn!
I sent all the boys to Ann Arbor, all the girls to Rockford,
The while my life went on, getting more riches and honors –
Resting under my cedar tree at evening.
The years went on.
I sent the girls to Europe;   10
I dowered them when married.
I gave the boys money to start in business.
They were strong children, promising as apples
Before the bitten places show.
But John fled the country in disgrace.
Jenny died in childbirth –
I sat under my cedar tree.
Harry killed himself after a debauch,
Susan was divorced –
I sat under my cedar tree.   20
Paul was invalided from over-study,
Mary became a recluse at home for love of a man –
I sat under my cedar tree.
All were gone, or broken-winged or devoured by life –
I sat under my cedar tree.
My mate, the mother of them, was taken –
I sat under my cedar tree,
Till ninety years were tolled.
O maternal Earth, which rocks the fallen leaf to sleep.

Passer-by,
To love is to find your own soul
Through the soul of the beloved one.
When the beloved one withdraws itself from your soul
Then you have lost your soul.
It is written: 'I have a friend,
But my sorrow has no friend.'
Hence my long years of solitude at the home of my father,
Trying to get myself back,
And to turn my sorrow into a supremer self.   10
But there was my father with his sorrows,
Sitting under the cedar tree,
A picture that sank into my heart at last
Bringing infinite repose.
Oh, ye souls who have made life
Fragrant and white as tube roses
From earth's dark soil,
Eternal peace!

Daniel M'Cumber

When I went to the city, Mary McNeely,
I meant to return for you, yes I did.
But Laura, my landlady's daughter,
Stole into my life somehow, and won me away.
Then after some years whom should I meet
But Georgine Miner from Niles – a sprout
Of the free love, Fourierist gardens that flourished
Before the war all over Ohio.
Her dilettante lover had tired of her,
And she turned to me for strength and solace.   10
She was some kind of a crying thing
One takes in one's arms, and all at once
It slimes your face with its running nose,
And voids its essence all over you,
Then bites your hand and springs away.
And there you stand bleeding and smelling to heaven!
Why, Mary McNeely, I was not worthy
To kiss the hem of your robe!

A stepmother drove me from home, embittering me.
A squaw-man, a flaneur and dilettante took my virtue.
For years I was his mistress – no one knew.
I learned from him the parasite cunning
With which I moved with the bluffs, like a flea on a dog.
All the time I was nothing but 'very private', with different men.
Then Daniel, the radical, had me for years.
His sister called me his mistress,
And Daniel wrote me: 'Shameful word, soiling our beautiful love!'
But my anger coiled, preparing its fangs.   10
My Lesbian friend next took a hand.
She hated Daniel's sister.
And Daniel despised her midget husband.
And she saw a chance for a poisonous thrust:
I must complain to the wife of Daniel's pursuit!
But before I did that I begged him to fly to London with me.
'Why not stay in the city just as we have?' he asked.
Then I turned submarine and revenged his repulse
In the arms of my dilettante friend. Then up to the surface,
Bearing the letter that Daniel wrote me,   20
To prove my honor was all intact, showing it to his wife,
My Lesbian friend and everyone.
If Daniel had only shot me dead!
Instead of stripping me naked of lies
A harlot in body and soul.

Very well, you liberals,
And navigators into realms intellectual,
You sailors through heights imaginative,
Blown about by erratic currents, tumbling into air pockets,
You Margaret Fuller Slacks, Petits,
And Tennessee Claflin Shopes –
You found with all your boasted wisdom
How hard at the last it is
To keep the soul from splitting into cellular atoms.
While we, seekers of earth's treasures   10
Getters and hoarders of gold,
Are self-contained, compact, harmonized,
Even to the end.

Penniwit, the Artist

I lost my patronage in Spoon River
From trying to put my mind in the camera
To catch the soul of the person.
The very best picture I ever took
Was of Judge Somers, attorney at law.
He sat upright and had me pause
Till he got his cross-eye straight.
Then when he was ready he said 'all right.'
And I yelled 'overruled' and his eye turned up.
And I caught him just as he used to look 10
When saying 'I except.'

Jim Brown

While I was handling Dom Pedro
I got at the thing that divides the race between men who are
For singing 'Turkey in the straw' or 'There is a fountain filled with blood' –
(Like Rile Potter used to sing it over at Concord);
For cards, or for Revd Peet's lecture on the holy land;
For skipping the light fantastic, or passing the plate;
For *Pinafore*, or a Sunday school cantata;
For men, or for money;
For the people or against them.
This was it: Revd Peet and the Social Purity Club,   10
Headed by Ben Pantier's wife,
Went to the Village trustees,
And asked them to make me take Dom Pedro
From the barn of Wash McNeely, there at the edge of town,
To a barn outside of the corporation,
On the ground that it corrupted public morals.
Well, Ben Pantier and Fiddler Jones saved the day –
They thought it a slam on colts.

I grew spiritually fat living off the souls of men.
If I saw a soul that was strong
I wounded its pride and devoured its strength.
The shelters of friendship knew my cunning,
For where I could steal a friend I did so.
And wherever I could enlarge my power
By undermining ambition, I did so,
Thus to make smooth my own.
And to triumph over other souls,
Just to assert and prove my superior strength,   10
Was with me a delight,
The keen exhilaration of soul gymnastics.
Devouring souls, I should have lived forever.
But their undigested remains bred in me a deadly nephritis,
With fear, restlessness, sinking spirits,
Hatred, suspicion, vision disturbed.
I collapsed at last with a shriek.
Remember the acorn:
It does not devour other acorns.

Elsa Wertman

I was a peasant girl from Germany,
Blue-eyed, rosy, happy and strong.
And the first place I worked was at Thomas Greene's.
On a summer's day when she was away
He stole into the kitchen and took me
Right in his arms and kissed me on my throat,
I turning my head. Then neither of us
Seemed to know what happened.
And I cried for what would become of me.
And cried and cried as my secret began to show.   10
One day Mrs Greene said she understood,
And would make no trouble for me,
And, being childless, would adopt it.
(He had given her a farm to be still.)
So she hid in the house and sent out rumors,
As if it were going to happen to her.
And all went well and the child was born – They were so kind to me.
Later I married Gus Wertman, and years passed.
But – at political rallies when sitters-by thought I was crying
At the eloquence of Hamilton Greene –   20
That was not it.
No! I wanted to say:
That's my son! That's my son!

Hamilton Greene

I was the only child of Frances Harris of Virginia
And Thomas Greene of Kentucky,
Of valiant and honorable blood both.
To them I owe all that I became,
Judge, member of Congress, leader in the State.
From my mother I inherited
Vivacity, fancy, language;
From my father will, judgment, logic.
All honor to them
For what service I was to the people!   10

Ernest Hyde

My mind was a mirror:
It saw what it saw, it knew what it knew.
In youth my mind was just a mirror
In a rapidly flying car,
Which catches and loses bits of the landscape.
Then in time
Great scratches were made on the mirror,
Letting the outside world come in,
And letting my inner self look out.
For this is the birth of the soul in sorrow,   10
A birth with gains and losses.
The mind sees the world as a thing apart,
And the soul makes the world at one with itself.
A mirror scratched reflects no image –
And this is the silence of wisdom.

Oh many times did Ernest Hyde and I
Argue about the freedom of the will.
My favorite metaphor was Prickett's cow
Roped out to grass, and free, you know, as far
As the length of the rope.
One day while arguing so, watching the cow
Pull at the rope to get beyond the circle
Which she had eaten bare,
Out came the stake, and tossing up her head,
She ran for us.   10
'What's that, free will or what?' said Ernest, running.
I fell just as she gored me to my death.

Amos Sibley

Not character, not fortitude, not patience
Were mine, the which the village thought I had
In bearing with my wife, while preaching on,
Doing the work God chose for me.
I loathed her as a termagant, as a wanton.
I knew of her adulteries, every one.
But even so, if I divorced the woman
I must forsake the ministry.
Therefore to do God's work and have it crop,
I bore with her!   10
So lied I to myself!
So lied I to Spoon River!
Yet I tried lecturing, ran for the legislature,
Canvassed for books, with just the thought in mind:
If I make money thus,
I will divorce her.

Mrs Sibley

The secret of the stars,– gravitation.
The secret of the earth,– layers of rock.
The secret of the soil,– to receive seed.
The secret of the seed, – the germ.
The secret of man,– the sower.
The secret of woman,– the soil.
My secret: Under a mound that you shall never find.

Adam Weirauch

I was crushed between Altgeld and Armour[3].
I lost many friends, much time and money
Fighting for Altgeld whom Editor Whedon
Denounced as the candidate of gamblers and anarchists.
Then Armour started to ship dressed meat to Spoon River,
Forcing me to shut down my slaughterhouse
And my butcher shop went all to pieces.
The new forces of Altgeld and Armour caught me
At the same time.
I thought it due me, to recoup the money I lost   10
And to make good the friends that left me,
For the Governor to appoint me Canal Commissioner.
Instead he appointed Whedon of the Spoon River *Argus*,
So I ran for the legislature and was elected.
I said to hell with principle and sold my vote
On Charles T. Yerkes' street-car franchise.
Of course I was one of the fellows they caught.
Who was it, Armour, Altgeld or myself
That ruined me?

A chaplain in the army,
A chaplain in the prisons,
An exhorter in Spoon River,
Drunk with divinity, Spoon River –
Yet bringing poor Eliza Johnson to shame,
And myself to scorn and wretchedness.
But why will you never see that love of women,
And even love of wine,
Are the stimulants by which the soul, hungering for divinity,
Reaches the ecstatic vision   10
And sees the celestial outposts?
Only after many trials for strength,
Only when all stimulants fail,
Does the aspiring soul
By its own sheer power
Find the divine
By resting upon itself.

Amelia Garrick

Yes, here I lie close to a stunted rose bush
In a forgotten place near the fence
Where the thickets from Siever's woods
Have crept over, growing sparsely.
And you, you are a leader in New York,
The wife of a noted millionaire,
A name in the society columns,
Beautiful, admired, magnified perhaps
By the mirage of distance.
You have succeeded, I have failed   10
In the eyes of the world.
You are alive, I am dead.
Yet I know that I vanquished your spirit.
And I know that lying here far from you,
Unheard of among your great friends
In the brilliant world where you move,
I am really the unconquerable power over your life
That robs it of complete triumph.

John Hancock Otis

As to democracy, fellow citizens,
Are you not prepared to admit
That I, who inherited riches and was to the manor born,
Was second to none in Spoon River
In my devotion to the cause of Liberty?
While my contemporary, Anthony Findlay,
Born in a shanty and beginning life
As a water carrier to the section hands,
Then becoming a section hand when he was grown,
Afterwards foreman of the gang, until he rose   10
To the superintendency of the railroad,
Living in Chicago,
Was a veritable slave driver,
Grinding the faces of labor,
And a bitter enemy of democracy.
And I say to you, Spoon River,
And to you, O republic,
Beware of the man who rises to power
From one suspender.

The Unknown

Ye aspiring ones, listen to the story of the unknown
Who lies here with no stone to mark the place.
As a boy reckless and wanton,
Wandering with gun in hand through the forest
Near the mansion of Aaron Hatfield,
I shot a hawk perched on the top
Of a dead tree.
He fell with guttural cry
At my feet, his wing broken.
Then I put him in a cage   10
Where he lived many days cawing angrily at me
When I offered him food.
Daily I search the realms of Hades
For the soul of the hawk,
That I may offer him the friendship
Of one whom life wounded and caged.

Alexander Throckmorton

In youth my wings were strong and tireless,
But I did not know the mountains.
In age I knew the mountains
But my weary wings could not follow my vision –
Genius is wisdom and youth.

Jonathan Swift Somers

After you have enriched your soul
To the highest point,
With books, thought, suffering, the understanding of many personalities,
The power to interpret glances, silences,
The pauses in momentous transformations,
The genius of divination and prophecy;
So that you feel able at times to hold the world
In the hollow of your hand,
Then, if, by the crowding of so many powers
Into the compass of your soul,   10
Your soul takes fire,
And in the conflagration of your soul
The evil of the world is lighted up and made clear –
Be thankful if in that hour of supreme vision
Life does not fiddle.

Widow McFarlane

I was the widow McFarlane,
Weaver of carpets for all the village.
And I pity you still at the loom of life,
You who are singing to the shuttle
And lovingly watching the work of your hands,
If you reach the day of hate, of terrible truth.
For the cloth of life is woven, you know,
To a pattern hidden under the loom –
A pattern you never see!
And you weave high-hearted, singing, singing,   10
You guard the threads of love and friendship
For noble figures in gold and purple.
And long after other eyes can see
You have woven a moon-white strip of cloth,
You laugh in your strength, for Hope o'erlays it
With shapes of love and beauty.
The loom stops short! The pattern's out!
You're alone in the room! You have woven a shroud!
And hate of it lays you in it!

Carl Hamblin

The press of the Spoon River *Clarion* was wrecked,
And I was tarred and feathered,
For publishing this on the day the Anarchists were hanged in Chicago:
'I saw a beautiful woman with bandaged eyes
Standing on the steps of a marble temple.
Great multitudes passed in front of her,
Lifting their faces to her imploringly.
In her left hand she held a sword.
She was brandishing the sword,
Sometimes striking a child, again a laborer,   10
Again a slinking woman, again a lunatic.
In her right hand she held a scale.
Into the scale pieces of gold were tossed
By those who dodged the strokes of the sword.
A man in a black gown read from a manuscript:
"She is no respecter of persons."
Then a youth wearing a red cap
Leaped to her side and snatched away the bandage.
And lo, the lashes had been eaten away
From the oozy eyelids;   20
The eyeballs were seared with a milky mucus:
The madness of a dying soul
Was written on her face –
But the multitude saw why she wore the bandage.'

To be able to see every side of every question,
To be on every side, to be everything, to be nothing long,
To pervert truth, to ride it for a purpose,
To use great feelings and passions of the human family
For base designs, for cunning ends,
To wear a mask like the Greek actors –
Your eight-page paper – behind which you huddle,
Bawling through the megaphone of big type:
'This is I, the giant.'
Thereby also living the life of a sneak-thief,   10
Poisoned with the anonymous words
Of your clandestine soul.
To scratch dirt over scandal for money,
And exhume it to the winds for revenge,
Or to sell papers,
Crushing reputations, or bodies, if need be,
To win at any cost, save your own life.
To glory in demoniac power, ditching civilization,
As a paranoiac boy puts a log on the track
And derails the express train.   20
To be an editor, as I was.
Then to lie here close by the river over the place
Where the sewage flows from the village,
And the empty cans and garbage are dumped,
And abortions are hidden.

Eugene Carman

Rhodes' slave! Selling shoes and gingham,
Flour and bacon, overalls, clothing, all day long
For fourteen hours a day for three hundred and thirteen days
For more than twenty years.
Saying 'Yes'm' and 'Yes, sir', and 'Thank you'
A thousand times a day, and all for fifty dollars a month.
Living in this stinking room in the rattle-trap 'Commercial.'
And compelled to go to Sunday School, and to listen
To the Revd Abner Peet one hundred and four times a year
For more than an hour at a time,   10
Because Thomas Rhodes ran the church
As well as the store and the bank.
So while I was tying my necktie that morning
I suddenly saw myself in the glass:
My hair all gray, my face like a sodden pie.
So I cursed and cursed: You damned old thing
You cowardly dog! You rotten pauper!
You Rhodes' slave! Till Roger Baughman
Thought I was having a fight with someone,
And looked through the transom just in time   20
To see me fall on the floor in a heap
From a broken vein in my head.

Clarence Fawcett

The sudden death of Eugene Carman
Put me in line to be promoted to fifty dollars a month,
And I told my wife and children that night.
But it didn't come, and so I thought
Old Rhodes suspected me of stealing
The blankets I took and sold on the side
For money to pay a doctor's bill for my little girl.
Then like a bolt old Rhodes accused me,
And promised me mercy for my family's sake
If I confessed, and so I confessed,   10
And begged him to keep it out of the papers,
And I asked the editors, too.
That night at home the constable took me
And every paper, except the *Clarion*,
Wrote me up as a thief
Because old Rhodes was an advertiser
And wanted to make an example of me.
Oh! well, you know how the children cried,
And how my wife pitied and hated me,
And how I came to lie here.   20

W. Lloyd Garrison Standard

Vegetarian, non-resistant, freethinker, in ethics a Christian,
Orator apt at the rhinestone rhythm of Ingersoll.
Carnivorous, avenger, believer and pagan.
Continent, promiscuous, changeable, treacherous, vain,
Proud, with the pride that makes struggle a thing for laughter.
With heart cored out by the worm of theatric despair,
Wearing the coat of indifference to hide the shame of defeat,
I, child of the abolitionist idealism –
A sort of Brand[4] in a birth of half-and-half.
What other thing could happen when I defended   10
The patriot scamps who burned the courthouse
That Spoon River might have a new one
Than plead them guilty? When Kinsey Keene drove through
The cardboard mask of my life with a spear of light,
What could I do but slink away, like the beast of myself
Which I raised from a whelp, to a corner and growl?
The pyramid of my life was nought but a dune,
Barren and formless, spoiled at last by the storm.

Everyone laughed at Col. Prichard
For buying an engine so powerful
That it wrecked itself, and wrecked the grinder
He ran it with.
But here is a joke of cosmic size:
The urge of nature that made a man
Evolve from his brain a spiritual life –
O miracle of the world! –
The very same brain with which the ape and wolf
Get food and shelter and procreate themselves.   10
Nature has made man do this,
In a world where she gives him nothing to do
After all – (though the strength of his soul goes round
In a futile waste of power.
To gear itself to the mills of the gods) –
But get food and shelter and procreate himself!

Ralph Rhodes

All they said was true:
I wrecked my father's bank with my loans
To dabble in wheat, but this was true –
I was buying wheat for him as well,
Who couldn't margin the deal in his name
Because of his church relationship.
And while George Reece was serving his term
I chased the will-o'-the-wisp of women
And the mockery of wine in New York.
It's deathly to sicken of wine and women   10
When nothing else is left in life.
But suppose your head is gray, and bowed
On a table covered with acrid stubs
Of cigarettes and empty glasses,
And a knock is heard, and you know it's the knock
So long drowned out by popping corks
And the peacock screams of demireps –
And you look up, and there's your Theft,
Who waited until your head was gray,
And your heart skipped beats to say to you: 20
'The game is ended. I've called for you,
Go out on Broadway and be run over,
They'll ship you back to Spoon River.'

Mickey M'Grew

It was just like everything else in life:
Something outside myself drew me down,
My own strength never failed me.
Why, there was the time I earned the money
With which to go away to school,
And my father suddenly needed help
And I had to give him all of it.
Just so it went till I ended up
A man-of-all-work in Spoon River.
Thus when I got the water tower cleaned,   10
And they hauled me up the seventy feet,
I unhooked the rope from my waist,
And laughingly flung my giant arms
Over the smooth steel lips of the top of the tower –
But they slipped from the treacherous slime,
And down, down, down, I plunged
Through bellowing darkness!

Rosie Roberts

I was sick, but more than that, I was mad
At the crooked police, and the crooked game of life.
So I wrote to the Chief of Police at Peoria:
'I am here in my girlhood home in Spoon River,
Gradually wasting away.
But come and take me, I killed the son
Of the merchant prince, in Madam Lou's,
And the papers that said he killed himself
In his home while cleaning a hunting gun –
Lied like the devil to hush up scandal,   10
For the bribe of advertising.
In my room I shot him, at Madam Lou's,
Because he knocked me down when I said
That, in spite of all the money he had,
I'd see my lover that night.'

I staggered on through darkness,
There was a hazy sky, a few stars
Which I followed as best I could.
It was nine o'clock, I was trying to get home.
But somehow I was lost,
Though really keeping the road.
Then I reeled through a gate and into a yard,
And called at the top of my voice:
'Oh, Fiddler! Oh, Mr Jones!'
(I thought it was his house and he would show me the way home.)   10
But who should step out but A.D. Blood,
In his nightshirt, waving a stick of wood,
And roaring about the cursed saloons,
And the criminals they made?
'You drunken Oscar Hummel,' he said,
As I stood there weaving to and fro,
Taking the blows from the stick in his hand
Till I dropped down dead at his feet.

Josiah Tompkins

I was well known and much beloved
And rich, as fortunes are reckoned
In Spoon River, where I had lived and worked.
That was the home for me,
Though all my children had flown afar –
Which is the way of Nature – all but one.
The boy, who was the baby, stayed at home,
To be my help in my failing years
And the solace of his mother.
But I grew weaker, as he grew stronger,   10
And he quarreled with me about the business,
And his wife said I was a hindrance to it;
And he won his mother to see as he did,
Till they tore me up to be transplanted
With them to her girlhood home in Missouri.
And so much of my fortune was gone at last,
Though I made the will just as he drew it,
He profited little by it.

She loved me. Oh! how she loved me!
I never had a chance to escape
From the day she first saw me.
But then after we were married I thought
She might prove her mortality and let me out,
Or she might divorce me.
But few die, none resign.
Then I ran away and was gone a year on a lark.
But she never complained. She said all would be well,
That I would return. And I did return.   10
I told her that while taking a row in a boat
I had been captured near Van Buren Street
By pirates on Lake Michigan,
And kept in chains, so I could not write her.
She cried and kissed me, and said it was cruel,
Outrageous, inhuman!
I then concluded our marriage
Was a divine dispensation
And could not be dissolved,
Except by death.   20
I was right.

Mrs Purkapile

He ran away and was gone for a year.
When he came home he told me the silly story
Of being kidnapped by pirates on Lake Michigan
And kept in chains so he could not write me.
I pretended to believe it, though I knew very well
What he was doing, and that he met
The milliner, Mrs Williams, now and then
When she went to the city to buy goods, as she said.
But a promise is a promise
And marriage is marriage,   10
And out of respect for my own character
I refused to be drawn into a divorce
By the scheme of a husband who had merely grown tired
Of his marital vow and duty.

Mrs Kessler

Mr Kessler, you know, was in the army,
And he drew six dollars a month as a pension,
And stood on the corner talking politics,
Or sat at home reading Grant's *Memoirs*.
And I supported the family by washing,
Learning the secrets of all the people
From their curtains, counterpanes, shirts and skirts.
For things that are new grow old at length,
They're replaced with better or none at all:
People are prospering or falling back.   10
And rents and patches widen with time,
No thread or needle can pace decay,
And there are stains that baffle soap,
And there are colors that run in spite of you,
Blamed though you are for spoiling a dress.
Handkerchiefs, napery, have their secrets –
The laundress, Life, knows all about it.
And I, who went to all the funerals
Held in Spoon River, swear I never
Saw a dead face without thinking it looked   20
Like something washed and ironed.

Harmon Whitney

Out of the lights and roar of cities,
Drifting down like a spark in Spoon River,
Burnt out with the fire of drink, and broken,
The paramour of a woman I took in self-contempt,
But to hide a wounded pride as well.
To be judged and loathed by a village of little minds –
I, gifted with tongues and wisdom,
Sunk here to the dust of the justice court,
A picker of rags in the rubbage of spites and wrongs, –
I, whom fortune smiled on!   10
I in a village,
Spouting to gaping yokels pages of verse,
Out of the lore of golden years,
Or raising a laugh with a flash of filthy wit
When they bought the drinks to kindle my dying mind.
To be judged by you,
The soul of me hidden from you,
With its wound gangrened
By love for a wife who made the wound,
With her cold white bosom, treasonous, pure and hard,   20
Relentless to the last, when the touch of her hand,
At any time, might have cured me of the typhus,
Caught in the jungle of life where many are lost.
And only to think that my soul could not react,
Like Byron's did, in song, in something noble,
But turned on itself like a tortured snake –
Judge me this way, O world!

Bert Kessler

I winged my bird,
Though he flew toward the setting sun,
But just as the shot rang out, he soared
Up and up through the splinters of golden light,
Till he turned right over, feathers ruffled,
With some of the down of him floating near,
And fell like a plummet into the grass.
I tramped about, parting the tangles,
Till I saw a splash of blood on a stump,
And the quail lying close to the rotten roots.   10
I reached my hand, but saw no brier,
But something pricked and stung and numbed it.
And then, in a second, I spied the rattler –
The shutters wide in his yellow eyes,
The head of him arched, sunk back in the rings of him,
A circle of filth, the color of ashes,
Or oak leaves bleached under layers of leaves.
I stood like a stone as he shrank and uncoiled
And started to crawl beneath the stump,
When I fell limp in the grass.   20

Lambert Hutchins

I have two monuments besides this granite obelisk:
One, the house I built on the hill,
With its spires, bay windows, and roof of slate.
The other, the lakefront in Chicago,
Where the railroad keeps a switching yard,
With whistling engines and crunching wheels,
And smoke and soot thrown over the city,
And the crash of cars along the boulevard, –
A blot like a hog-pen on the harbor
Of a great metropolis, foul as a sty.   10
I helped to give this heritage
To generations yet unborn, with my vote
In the House of Representatives,
And the lure of the thing was to be at rest
From the never-ending fright of need,
And to give my daughters gentle breeding,
And a sense of security in life.
But, you see, though I had the mansion house
And traveling passes and local distinction,
I could hear the whispers, whispers, whispers,   20
Wherever I went, and my daughters grew up
With a look as if someone were about to strike them,
And they married madly, helter-skelter,
Just to get out and have a change.
And what was the whole of the business worth?
Why, it wasn't worth a damn!

I was the daughter of Lambert Hutchins,
Born in a cottage near the gristmill,
Reared in the mansion there on the hill,
With its spires, bay windows, and roof of slate.
How proud my mother was of the mansion!
How proud of father's rise in the world!
And how my father loved and watched us,
And guarded our happiness.
But I believe the house was a curse,
For father's fortune was little beside it;   10
And when my husband found he had married
A girl who was really poor,
He taunted me with the spires,
And called the house a fraud on the world,
A treacherous lure to young men, raising hopes
Of a dowry not to be had,
And a man while selling his vote
Should get enough from the people's betrayal
To wall the whole of his family in.
He vexed my life till I went back home   20
And lived like an old maid till I died,
Keeping house for father.

Hortense Robbins

My name used to be in the papers daily
As having dined somewhere,
Or traveled somewhere,
Or rented a house in Paris,
Where I entertained the nobility.
I was forever eating or traveling,
Or taking the cure at Baden-Baden.
Now I am here to do honor
To Spoon River, here beside the family whence I sprang.
No one cares now where I dined,   10
Or lived, or whom I entertained,
Or how often I took the cure at Baden-Baden.

Jacob Godbey

How did you feel, you libertarians,
Who spent your talents rallying noble reasons
Around the saloon, as if Liberty
Was not to be found anywhere except at the bar
Or at a table, guzzling?
How did you feel, Ben Pantier, and the rest of you,
Who almost stoned me for a tyrant,
Garbed as a moralist,
And as a wry-faced ascetic frowning upon Yorkshire pudding,
Roast beef and ale and good will and rosy cheer –   10
Things you never saw in a grog-shop in your life?
How did you feel after I was dead and gone,
And your goddess, Liberty, unmasked as a strumpet,
Selling out the streets of Spoon River
To the insolent giants
Who manned the saloons from afar?
Did it occur to you that personal liberty
Is liberty of the mind,
Rather than of the belly?

Walter Simmons

My parents thought that I would be
As great as Edison or greater,
For as a boy I made balloons
And wondrous kites and toys with clocks
And little engines with tracks to run on
And telephones of cans and thread.
I played the cornet and painted pictures,
Modeled in clay and took the part
Of the villain in the *Octoroon*.
But then at twenty-one I married   10
And had to live, and so, to live
I learned the trade of making watches
And kept the jewelry store on the square,
Thinking, thinking, thinking, thinking, –
Not of business, but of the engine
I studied the calculus to build.
And all Spoon River watched and waited
To see it work, but it never worked.
And a few kind souls believed my genius
Was somehow hampered by the store.   20
It wasn't true.
The truth was this:
I didn't have the brains.

Tom Beatty

I was a lawyer like Harmon Whitney
Or Kinsey Keene or Garrison Standard,
For I tried the rights of property,
Although by lamplight, for thirty years,
In that poker room in the opera house.
And I say to you that Life's a gambler
Head and shoulders above us all.
No mayor alive can close the house.
And if you lose, you can squeal as you will,
You'll not get back your money.   10
He makes the percentage hard to conquer,
He stacks the cards to catch your weakness
And not to meet your strength.
And he gives you seventy years to play:
For if you cannot win in seventy
You cannot win at all.
So, if you lose, get out of the room –
Get out of the room when your time is up.
It's mean to sit and fumble the cards
And curse your losses, leaden-eyed,   20
Whining to try and try.

Roy Butler

If the learned Supreme Court of Illinois
Got at the secret of every case
As well as it does a case of rape
It would be the greatest court in the world.
A jury, of neighbors mostly, with 'Butch' Weldy
As foreman, found me guilty in ten minutes
And two ballots on a case like this:
Richard Bandle and I had trouble over a fence,
And my wife and Mrs Bandle quarreled
As to whether Ipava was a finer town than Table Grove.   10
I awoke one morning with the love of God
Brimming over my heart, so I went to see Richard
To settle the fence in the spirit of Jesus Christ.
I knocked on the door, and his wife opened.
She smiled and asked me in. I entered –
She slammed the door and began to scream,
'Take your hands off, you low-down varlet!'
Just then her husband entered.
I waved my hands, choked up with words.
He went for his gun, and I ran out.   20
But neither the Supreme Court nor my wife
Believed a word she said.

I wanted to go away to college
But rich Aunt Persis wouldn't help me.
So I made gardens and raked the lawns
And bought John Alden's books[5] with my earnings
And toiled for the very means of life.
I wanted to marry Delia Prickett,
But how could I do it with what I earned?
And there was Aunt Persis more than seventy
Who sat in a wheelchair half alive
With her throat so paralyzed, when she swallowed   10
The soup ran out of her mouth like a duck –
A gourmand yet, investing her income
In mortgages, fretting all the time
About her notes and rents and papers.
That day I was sawing wood for her,
And reading Proudhon in between.
I went in the house for a drink of water,
And there she sat asleep in her chair,
And Proudhon lying on the table,
And a bottle of chloroform on the book,   20
She used sometimes for an aching tooth!
I poured the chloroform on a handkerchief
And held it to her nose till she died. –
Oh Delia, Delia, you and Proudhon
Steadied my hand, and the coroner
Said she died of heart failure.
I married Delia and got the money –
A joke on you, Spoon River?

Edmund Pollard

I would I had thrust my hands of flesh
Into the disk-flowers bee-infested,
Into the mirror-like core of fire
Of the light of life, the sun of delight.
For what are anthers worth or petals
Or halo-rays? Mockeries, shadows
Of the heart of the flower, the central flame!
All is yours, young passer-by.
Enter the banquet room with the thought,
Don't sidle in as if you were doubtful   10
Whether you're welcome – the feast is yours!
Nor take but a little, refusing more
With a bashful 'Thank you', when you're hungry.
Is your soul alive? Then let it feed!
Leave no balconies where you can climb,
Nor milk-white bosoms where you can rest,
Nor golden heads with pillows to share,
Nor wine cups while the wine is sweet,
Nor ecstasies of body or soul.
You will die, no doubt, but die while living   20
In depths of azure, rapt and mated,
Kissing the queen-bee, Life!

Thomas Trevelyan

Reading in Ovid the sorrowful story of Itys,
Son of the love of Tereus and Procne, slain
For the guilty passion of Tereus for Philomela,
The flesh of him served to Tereus by Procne,
And the wrath of Tereus, the murderess pursuing
Till the gods made Philomela a nightingale,
Lute of the rising moon, and Procne a swallow!
Oh livers and artists of Hellas centuries gone,
Sealing in little thuribles dreams and wisdom,
Incense beyond all price, forever fragrant,   10
A breath whereof makes clear the eyes of the soul!
How I inhaled its sweetness here in Spoon River!
The thurible opening when I had lived and learned
How all of us kill the children of love, and all of us,
Knowing not what we do, devour their flesh,
And all of us change to singers, although it be
But once in our lives, or change – alas! – to swallows,
To twitter amid cold winds and falling leaves!

Observe the clasped hands!
Are they hands of farewell or greeting,
Hands that I helped or hands that helped me?
Would it not be well to carve a hand
With an inverted thumb, like Elagabalus?
And yonder is a broken chain,
The weakest-link idea perhaps –
But what was it?
And lambs, some lying down,
Others standing, as if listening to the shepherd –   10
Others bearing a cross, one foot lifted up –
Why not chisel a few shambles?
And fallen columns! Carve the pedestal, please,
Or the foundations, let us see the cause of the fall.
And compasses and mathematical instruments,
In irony of the under-tenants' ignorance
Of determinants and the calculus of variations.
And anchors, for those who never sailed.
And gates ajar – yes, so they were:
You left them open and stray goats entered your garden.   20
And an eye watching like one of the Arimaspi[6] –
So did you – with one eye.
And angels blowing trumpets – you are heralded –
It is your horn and your angel and your family's estimate.
It is all very well, but for myself
I know I stirred certain vibrations in Spoon River
Which are my true epitaph, more lasting than stone.

Hiram Scates

I tried to win the nomination
For president of the County Board
And I made speeches all over the County
Denouncing Solomon Purple, my rival,
As an enemy of the people,
In league with the master-foes of man.
Young idealists, broken warriors,
Hobbling on one crutch of hope,
Souls that stake their all on the truth,
Losers of worlds at heaven's bidding,   10
Flocked about me and followed my voice
As the savior of the County.
But Solomon won the nomination,
And then I faced about,
And rallied my followers to his standard,
And made him victor, made him King
Of the Golden Mountain with the door
Which closed on my heels just as I entered,
Flattered by Solomon's invitation,
To be the County Board's secretary.   20
And out in the cold stood all my followers:
Young idealists, broken warriors
Hobbling on one crutch of hope –
Souls that staked their all on the truth,
Losers of worlds at heaven's bidding,
Watching the Devil kick the Millennium[7]
Over the Golden Mountain.

Peleg Poague

Horses and men are just alike.
There was my stallion, Billy Lee,
Black as a cat and trim as a deer,
With an eye of fire, keen to start,
And he could hit the fastest speed
Of any racer around Spoon River.
But just as you'd think he couldn't lose,
With his lead of fifty yards or more,
He'd rear himself and throw the rider,
And fall back over, tangled up,   10
Completely gone to pieces.
You see he was a perfect fraud:
He couldn't win, he couldn't work,
He was too light to haul or plow with,
And no one wanted colts from him.
And when I tried to drive him – well,
He ran away and killed me.

Jeduthan Hawley

There would be a knock at the door
And I would arise at midnight and go to the shop,
Where belated travelers would hear me hammering
Sepulchral boards and tacking satin.
And often I wondered who would go with me
To the distant land, our names the theme
For talk, in the same week, for I've observed
Two always go together.
Chase Henry was paired with Edith Conant;
And Jonathan Somers with Willie Metcalf,   10
And Editor Hamblin with Francis Turner,
When he prayed to live longer than Editor Whedon,
And Thomas Rhodes with widow McFarlane,
And Emily Sparks with Barry Holden,
And Oscar Hummel with Davis Matlock,
And Editor Whedon with Fiddler Jones,
And Faith Matheny with Dorcas Gustine.
And l, the solemnest man in town,
Stepped off with Daisy Fraser.

Abel Melveny

I bought every kind of machine that's known –
Grinders, shellers, planters, mowers,
Mills and rakes and ploughs and threshers –
And all of them stood in the rain and sun,
Getting rusted, warped and battered,
For I had no sheds to store them in,
And no use for most of them.
And toward the last, when I thought it over,
There by my window, growing clearer
About myself, as my pulse slowed down,   10
And looked at one of the mills I bought –
Which I didn't have the slightest need of,
As things turned out, and I never ran –
A fine machine, once brightly varnished,
And eager to do its work,
Now with its paint washed off –
I saw myself as a good machine
That Life had never used.

My mother was for woman's rights
And my father was the rich miller at London Mills.
I dreamed of the wrongs of the world and wanted to right them.
When my father died, I set out to see peoples and countries
In order to learn how to reform the world.
I traveled through many lands.
I saw the ruins of Rome
And the ruins of Athens,
And the ruins of Thebes.
And I sat by moonlight amid the necropolis of Memphis.   10
There I was caught up by wings of flame,
And a voice from heaven said to me:
'Injustice, Untruth destroyed them. Go forth!
Preach Justice! Preach Truth!'
And I hastened back to Spoon River
To say farewell to my mother before beginning my work.
They all saw a strange light in my eye.
And by and by, when I talked, they discovered
What had come in my mind.
Then Jonathan Swift Somers challenged me to debate   20
The subject (I taking the negative):
'Pontius Pilate, the Greatest Philosopher of the World'.
And he won the debate by saying at last,
'Before you reform the world, Mr Tutt,
Please answer the question of Pontius Pilate:
"What is Truth?"'

Elliott Hawkins

I looked like Abraham Lincoln.
I was one of you, Spoon River, in all fellowship,
But standing for the rights of property and for order.
A regular church attendant,
Sometimes appearing in your town meetings to warn you
Against the evils of discontent and envy,
And to denounce those who tried to destroy the Union,
And to point to the peril of the Knights of Labor[7].
My success and my example are inevitable influences
In your young men and in generations to come,   10
In spite of attacks of newspapers like the *Clarion*;
A regular visitor at Springfield
When the Legislature was in session
To prevent raids upon the railroads
And the men building up the state.
Trusted by them and by you, Spoon River, equally
In spite of the whispers that I was a lobbyist.
Moving quietly through the world, rich and courted.
Dying at last, of course, but lying here
Under a stone with an open book carved upon it   20
And the words 'Of such is the Kingdom of Heaven.'
And now, you world-savers, who reaped nothing in life
And in death have neither stones nor epitaphs,
How do you like your silence from mouths stopped
With the dust of my triumphant career?

Enoch Dunlap

How many times, during the twenty years
I was your leader, friends of Spoon River,
Did you neglect the convention and caucus,
And leave the burden on my hands
Of guarding and saving the people's cause? –
Sometimes because you were ill,
Or your grandmother was ill,
Or you drank too much and fell asleep,
Or else you said: 'He is our leader,
All will be well; he fights for us,   10
We have nothing to do but follow.'
But oh, how you cursed me when I fell,
And cursed me, saying I had betrayed you,
In leaving the caucus room for a moment,
When the people's enemies, there assembled,
Waited and watched for a chance to destroy
The Sacred Rights of the People.
You common rabble! I left the caucus
To go to the urinal.

Ida Frickey

Nothing in life is alien to you:
I was a penniless girl from Summum
Who stepped from the morning train in Spoon River.
All the houses stood before me with closed doors
And drawn shades – I was barred out,
I had no place or part in any of them.
And I walked past the old McNeely mansion,
A castle of stone 'mid walks and gardens
With workmen about the place on guard
And the County and State upholding it   10
For its lordly owner, full of pride.
I was so hungry I had a vision:
I saw a giant pair of scissors
Dip from the sky, like the beam of a dredge,
And cut the house in two like a curtain.
But at the 'Commercial' I saw a man
Who winked at me as I asked for work –
It was Wash McNeely's son.
He proved the link in the chain of title
To half my ownership of the mansion,   20
Through a breach of promise suit – the scissors.
So, you see, the house, from the day I was born,
Was only waiting for me.

Seth Compton

When I died, the circulating library
Which I built up for Spoon River,
And managed for the good of inquiring minds,
Was sold at auction on the public square,
As if to destroy the last vestige
Of my memory and influence.
For those of you who could not see the virtue
Of knowing Volney's *Ruins* as well as Butler's *Analogy*
And *Faust* as well as *Evangeline*[9],
Were really the power in the village,   10
And often you asked me,
'What is the use of knowing the evil in the world?'
I am out of your way now, Spoon River.
Choose your own good and call it good.
For I could never make you see
That no one knows what is good
Who knows not what is evil,
And no one knows what is true
Who knows not what is false.

Felix Schmidt

It was only a little house of two rooms –
Almost like a child's playhouse –
With scarce five acres of ground around it;
And I had so many children to feed
And school and clothe, and a wife who was sick
From bearing children.
One day lawyer Whitney came along
And proved to me that Christian Dallman,
Who owned three thousand acres of land,
Had bought the eighty that adjoined me   10
In eighteen hundred and seventy-one
For eleven dollars, at a sale for taxes,
While my father lay in his mortal illness.
So the quarrel arose and I went to law.
But when we came to the proof,
A survey of the land showed clear as day
That Dallman's tax deed covered my ground
And my little house of two rooms.
It served me right for stirring him up.
I lost my case and lost my place.   20
I left the courtroom and went to work
As Christian Dallman's tenant.

Richard Bone

When I first came to Spoon River
I did not know whether what they told me
Was true or false.
They would bring me the epitaph
And stand around the shop while I worked
And say 'He was so kind,' 'He was so wonderful,'
'She was the sweetest woman,' 'He was a consistent Christian.'
And I chiseled for them whatever they wished,
All in ignorance of the truth.
But later, as I lived among the people here,   10
I knew how near to the life
Were the epitaphs that were ordered for them as they died.
But still I chiseled whatever they paid me to chisel
And made myself party to the false chronicles
Of the stones,
Even as the historian does who writes
Without knowing the truth,
Or because he is influenced to hide it.

Silas Dement

It was moonlight, and the earth sparkled
With new-fallen frost.
It was midnight and not a soul abroad.
Out of the chimney of the courthouse
A greyhound of smoke leapt and chased
The northwest wind.
I carried a ladder to the landing of the stairs
And leaned it against the frame of the trap-door
In the ceiling of the portico,
And I crawled under the roof and amid the rafters   10
And flung among the seasoned timbers
A lighted handful of oil-soaked waste.
Then I came down and slunk away.
In a little while the fire-bell rang –
Clang! Clang! Clang!
And the Spoon River ladder company
Came with a dozen buckets and began to pour water
On the glorious bonfire, growing hotter,
Higher and brighter, till the walls fell in,
And the limestone columns where Lincoln stood   20
Crashed like trees when the woodman fells them…
When I came back from Joliet
There was a new courthouse with a dome.
For I was punished like all who destroy
The past for the sake of the future.

Dillard Sissman

The buzzards wheel slowly
In wide circles, in a sky
Faintly hazed as from dust from the road.
And a wind sweeps through the pasture where I lie
Beating the grass into long waves.
My kite is above the wind,
Though now and then it wobbles,
Like a man shaking his shoulders,
And the tail streams out momentarily,
Then sinks to rest.   10
And the buzzards wheel and wheel,
Sweeping the zenith with wide circles
Above my kite. And the hills sleep.
And a farmhouse, white as snow,
Peeps from green trees – far away.
And I watch my kite,
For the thin moon will kindle herself ere long,
Then she will swing like a pendulum dial
To the tail of my kite.
A spurt of flame like a water-dragon   20
Dazzles my eyes –
I am shaken as a banner.

E.C. Culbertson

Is it true, Spoon River,
That in the hallway of the new courthouse
There is a tablet of bronze
Containing the embossed faces
Of Editor Whedon and Thomas Rhodes?
And is it true that my successful labors
In the County Board, without which
Not one stone would have been placed on another,
And the contributions out of my own pocket
To build the temple, are but memories among the people,   10
Gradually fading away, and soon to descend
With them to this oblivion where I lie?
In truth, I can so believe.
For it is a law of the Kingdom of Heaven
That whoso enters the vineyard at the eleventh hour
Shall receive a full day's pay.
And it is a law of the Kingdom of this World
That those who first oppose a good work
Seize it and make it their own,
When the cornerstone is laid,   20
And memorial tablets are erected.

Shack Dye

The white men played all sorts of jokes on me.
They took big fish off my hook
And put little ones on, while I was away
Getting a stringer, and made me believe
I hadn't seen aright the fish I had caught.
When Burr Robbins circus came to town
They got the ringmaster to let a tame leopard
Into the ring, and made me believe
I was whipping a wild beast like Samson
When l, for an offer of fifty dollars,   10
Dragged him out to his cage.
One time I entered my blacksmith shop
And shook as I saw some horseshoes crawling
Across the floor, as if alive –
Walter Simmons had put a magnet
Under the barrel of water.
Yet every one of you, you white men,
Was fooled about fish and about leopards too,
And you didn't know any more than the horseshoes did
What moved you about Spoon River.   20

Hildrup Tubbs

I made two fights for the people.
First I left my party, bearing the gonfalon
Of independence, for reform, and was defeated.
Next I used my rebel strength
To capture the standard of my old party –
And I captured it, but I was defeated.
Discredited and discarded, misanthropical,
I turned to the solace of gold
And I used my remnant of power
To fasten myself like a saprophyte   10
Upon the putrescent carcass
Of Thomas Rhodes' bankrupt bank,
As assignee of the fund.
Everyone now turned from me.
My hair grew white,
My purple lusts grew gray,
Tobacco and whisky lost their savor,
And for years Death ignored me
As he does a hog.

Henry Tripp

The bank broke and I lost my savings.
I was sick of the tiresome game in Spoon River
And I made up my mind to run away
And leave my place in life and my family,
But just as the midnight train pulled in,
Quick off the steps jumped Cully Green
And Martin Vise, and began to fight
To settle their ancient rivalry,
Striking each other with fists that sounded
Like the blows of knotted clubs.   10
Now it seemed to me that Cully was winning,
When his bloody face broke into a grin
Of sickly cowardice, leaning on Martin
And whining out, 'We're good friends, Mart,
You know that I'm your friend.'
But a terrible punch from Martin knocked him
Around and around and into a heap.
And then they arrested me as a witness,
And I lost my train and staid in Spoon River
To wage my battle of life to the end.   20
Oh, Cully Green, you were my savior –
You, so ashamed and drooped for years,
Loitering listless about the streets,
And tying rags round your festering soul,
Who failed to fight it out.

Granville Calhoun

I wanted to be County Judge
One more term, so as to round out a service
Of thirty years.
But my friends left me and joined my enemies,
And they elected a new man.
Then a spirit of revenge seized me,
And I infected my four sons with it,
And I brooded upon retaliation,
Until the great physician, Nature,
Smote me through with paralysis   10
To give my soul and body a rest.
Did my sons get power and money?
Did they serve the people or yoke them
To till and harvest fields of self?
For how could they ever forget
My face at my bedroom window,
Sitting helpless amid my golden cages
Of singing canaries,
Looking at the old courthouse?

Henry C. Calhoun

I reached the highest place in Spoon River,
But through what bitterness of spirit!
The face of my father, sitting speechless,
Childlike, watching his canaries,
And looking at the courthouse window
Of the County Judge's room,
And his admonitions to me to seek
My own in life, and punish Spoon River
To avenge the wrong the people did him,
Filled me with furious energy   10
To seek for wealth and seek for power.
But what did he do but send me along
The path that leads to the grove of the Furies?
I followed the path and I tell you this:
On the way to the grove you'll pass the Fates,
Shadow-eyed, bent over their weaving.
Stop for a moment, and if you see
The thread of revenge leap out of the shuttle
Then quickly snatch from Atropos
The shears and cut it, lest your sons,   20
And the children of them and their children,
Wear the envenomed robe.

Why was I not devoured by self-contempt,
And rotted down by indifference
And impotent revolt like Indignation Jones?
Why, with all of my errant steps
Did I miss the fate of Willard Fluke?
And why, though I stood at Burchard's bar,
As a sort of decoy for the house to the boys
To buy the drinks, did the curse of drink
Fall on me like rain that runs off,
Leaving the soul of me dry and clean?   10
And why did I never kill a man
Like Jack McGuire?
But instead I mounted a little in life,
And I owe it all to a book I read.
But why did I go to Mason City,
Where I chanced to see the book in a window,
With its garish cover luring my eye?
And why did my soul respond to the book,
As I read it over and over?[10]

Perry Zoll

My thanks, friends of the County Scientific Association,
For this modest boulder,
And its little tablet of bronze.
Twice I tried to join your honored body,
And was rejected,
And when my little brochure
On the intelligence of plants
Began to attract attention
You almost voted me in.
After that I grew beyond the need of you   10
And your recognition.
Yet I do not reject your memorial stone,
Seeing that I should, in so doing,
Deprive you of honor to yourselves.

Magrady Graham

Tell me, was Altgeld elected Governor?
For when the returns began to come in
And Cleveland was sweeping the East
It was too much for you, poor old heart,
Who had striven for democracy
In the long, long years of defeat.
And like a watch that is worn
I felt you growing slower until you stopped.
Tell me, was Altgeld elected,
And what did he do?   10
Did they bring his head on a platter to a dancer,
Or did he triumph for the people?
For when I saw him
And took his hand,
The childlike blueness of his eyes
Moved me to tears,
And there was an air of eternity about him,
Like the cold, clear light that rests at dawn
On the hills!

Archibald Higbie

I loathed you, Spoon River. I tried to rise above you,
I was ashamed of you. I despised you
As the place of my nativity.
And there in Rome, among the artists,
Speaking Italian, speaking French,
I seemed to myself at times to be free
Of every trace of my origin.
I seemed to be reaching the heights of art
And to breathe the air that the masters breathed
And to see the world with their eyes.   10
But still they'd pass my work and say,
'What are you driving at, my friend?
Sometimes the face looks like Apollo's
At others it has a trace of Lincoln's.'
There was no culture, you know, in Spoon River
And I burned with shame and held my peace.
And what could I do, all covered over
And weighted down with western soil
Except aspire, and pray for another
Birth in the world, with all of Spoon River   20
Rooted out of my soul?

Tom Merritt

At first I suspected something –
She acted so calm and absent-minded.
And one day I heard the back door shut
As I entered the front, and I saw him slink
Back of the smokehouse into the lot
And run across the field.
And I meant to kill him on sight.
But that day, walking near Fourth Bridge
Without a stick or a stone at hand,
All of a sudden I saw him standing   10
Scared to death, holding his rabbits,
And all I could say was, 'Don't, Don't, Don't,'
As he aimed and fired at my heart.

Mrs Merritt

Silent before the jury,
Returning no word to the judge when he asked me
If I had aught to say against the sentence,
Only shaking my head.
What could I say to people who thought
That a woman of thirty-five was at fault
When her lover of nineteen killed her husband?
Even though she had said to him over and over,
'Go away, Elmer, go far away,
I have maddened your brain with the gift of my body: 10
You will do some terrible thing.'
And just as I feared, he killed my husband,
With which I had nothing to do, before God!
Silent for thirty years in prison
And the iron gates of Joliet
Swung as the gray and silent trusties
Carried me out in a coffin.

Elmer Karr

What but the love of God could have softened
And made forgiving the people of Spoon River
Toward me who wronged the bed of Thomas Merritt
And murdered him beside?
Oh, loving hearts that took me in again
When I returned from fourteen years in prison!
Oh, helping hands that in the church received me,
And heard with tears my penitent confession,
Who took the sacrament of bread and wine!
Repent, ye living ones, and rest with Jesus.   10

Elizabeth Childers

Dust of my dust,
And dust with my dust,
O child who died as you entered the world,
Dead with my death!
Not knowing
Breath, though you tried so hard,
With a heart that beat when you lived with me,
And stopped when you left me for Life.
It is well, my child. For you never traveled
The long, long way that begins with school days,   10
When little fingers blur under the tears
That fall on the crooked letters.
And the earliest wound, when a little mate
Leaves you alone for another.
And sickness, and the face of Fear by the bed;
The death of a father or mother.
Or shame for them, or poverty.
The maiden sorrow of school days ended,
And eyeless Nature that makes you drink
From the cup of Love, though you know it's poisoned.   20
To whom would your flower-face have been lifted?
Botanist, weakling? Cry of what blood to yours? –
Pure or foul, for it makes no matter,
It's blood that calls to our blood.
And then your children – oh, what might they be?
And what your sorrow? Child! Child!
Death is better than Life.

Edith Conant

We stand about this place – we, the memories –
And shade our eyes because we dread to read:
'June 17th, 1884, aged 21 years and 3 days.'
And all things are changed.
And we – we, the memories – stand here for ourselves alone,
For no eye marks us, or would know why we are here.
Your husband is dead, your sister lives far away,
Your father is bent with age,
He has forgotten you, he scarcely leaves the house
Any more.   10
No one remembers your exquisite face,
Your lyric voice!
How you sang, even on the morning you were stricken,
With piercing sweetness, with thrilling sorrow,
Before the advent of the child which died with you.
It is all forgotten, save by us, the memories,
Who are forgotten by the world.
All is changed, save the river and the hill –
Even they are changed.
Only the burning sun and the quiet stars are the same.   20
And we – we, the memories – stand here in awe,
Our eyes closed with the weariness of tears –
In immeasurable weariness.

Father Malloy

You are over there, Father Malloy,
Where holy ground is, and the cross marks every grave,
Not here with us on the hill –
Us of wavering faith, and clouded vision,
And drifting hope, and unforgiven sins.
You were so human, Father Malloy,
Taking a friendly glass sometimes with us,
Siding with us who would rescue Spoon River
From the coldness and the dreariness of village morality.
You were like a traveler who brings a little box of sand   10
From the wastes about the pyramids
And makes them real and Egypt real.
You were a part of and related to a great past,
And yet you were so close to many of us.
You believed in the joy of life.
You did not seem to be ashamed of the flesh.
You faced life as it is,
And as it changes.
Some of us almost came to you, Father Malloy,
Seeing how your church had divined the heart,   20
And provided for it,
Through Peter the Flame,
Peter the Rock.

Ami Green

Not 'a youth with hoary head and haggard eye',
But an old man with a smooth skin
And black hair!
I had the face of a boy as long as I lived,
And for years a soul that was stiff and bent,
In a world which saw me just as a jest,
To be hailed familiarly when it chose,
And loaded up as a man when it chose,
Being neither man nor boy.
In truth it was soul as well as body   10
Which never matured, and I say to you
That the much-sought prize of eternal youth
Is just arrested growth.

Calvin Campbell

Ye who are kicking against Fate,
Tell me how it is that on this hillside
Running down to the river,
Which fronts the sun and the south wind,
This plant draws from the air and soil
Poison and becomes poison ivy?
And this plant draws from the same air and soil
Sweet elixirs and colors and becomes arbutus?
And both flourish?
You may blame Spoon River for what it is,   10
But whom do you blame for the will in you
That feeds itself and makes you dock-weed,
Jimpson, dandelion or mullen
And which can never use any soil or air
So as to make you jessamine or wistaria?

Henry Layton

Whoever thou art who passest by
Know that my father was gentle,
And my mother was violent,
While I was born the whole of such hostile halves,
Not intermixed and fused,
But each distinct, feebly soldered together.
Some of you saw me as gentle,
Some as violent,
Some as both.
But neither half of me wrought my ruin.   10
It was the falling asunder of halves,
Never a part of each other,
That left me a lifeless soul.

Harlan Sewall

You never understood, O unknown one,
Why it was I repaid
Your devoted friendship and delicate ministrations
First with diminished thanks,
Afterward by gradually withdrawing my presence from you,
So that I might not be compelled to thank you,
And then with silence which followed upon
Our final separation.
You had cured my diseased soul. But to cure it
You saw my disease, you knew my secret,   10
And that is why I fled from you.
For though when our bodies rise from pain
We kiss forever the watchful hands
That gave us wormwood, while we shudder
For thinking of the wormwood,
A soul that's cured is a different matter,
For there we'd blot from memory
The soft-toned words, the searching eyes,
And stand forever oblivious,
Not so much of the sorrow itself   20
As of the hand that healed it.

Ippolit Konovaloff

I was a gunsmith in Odessa.
One night the police broke in the room
Where a group of us were reading Spencer.
And seized our books and arrested us.
But I escaped and came to New York
And thence to Chicago, and then to Spoon River,
Where I could study my Kant in peace
And eke out a living repairing guns!
Look at my moulds! My architectonics!
One for a barrel, one for a hammer   10
And others for other parts of a gun!
Well, now suppose no gunsmith living
Had anything else but duplicate moulds
Of these I show you – well, all guns
Would be just alike, with a hammer to hit
The cap and a barrel to carry the shot,
All acting alike for themselves, and all
Acting against each other alike.
And there would be your world of guns!
Which nothing could ever free from itself   20
Except a Moulder with different moulds
To mould the metal over.

Henry Phipps

I was the Sunday School superintendent,
The dummy president of the wagon works
And the canning factory,
Acting for Thomas Rhodes and the banking clique,
My son the cashier of the bank,
Wedded to Rhodes' daughter,
My weekdays spent in making money,
My Sundays at church and in prayer.
In everything a cog in the wheel of things-as-they-are:
Of money, master and man, made white   10
With the paint of the Christian creed.
And then:
The bank collapsed. I stood and looked at the wrecked machine –
The wheels with blowholes stopped with putty and painted,
The rotten bolts, the broken rods,
And only the hopper for souls fit to be used again
In a new devourer of life,
When newspapers, judges and money-magicians
Build over again.
I was stripped to the bone, but I lay in the Rock of Ages,   20
Seeing now through the game, no longer a dupe,
And knowing 'the upright shall dwell in the land
But the years of the wicked shall be shortened.'
Then suddenly, Dr Meyers discovered
A cancer in my liver.
I was not, after all, the particular care of God!
Why, even thus standing on a peak
Above the mists through which I had climbed,
And ready for larger life in the world,
Eternal forces   30
Moved me on with a push.

I was just turned twenty-one,
And Henry Phipps, the Sunday School superintendent,
Made a speech in Bindle's Opera House.
'The honor of the flag must be upheld,' he said,
'Whether it be assailed by a barbarous tribe of Tagalogs
Or the greatest power in Europe.'
And we cheered and cheered the speech and the flag he waved
As he spoke.
And I went to the war in spite of my father,
And followed the flag till I saw it raised   10
By our camp in a rice field near Manila,
And all of us cheered and cheered it.
But there were flies and poisonous things,
And there was the deadly water,
And the cruel heat,
And the sickening, putrid food;
And the smell of the trench just back of the tents
Where the soldiers went to empty themselves,
And there were the whores who followed us, full of syphilis,
And beastly acts between ourselves or alone,   20
With bullying, hatred, degradation among us,
And days of loathing and nights of fear
To the hour of the charge through the steaming swamp,
Following the flag,
Till I fell with a scream, shot through the guts.
Now there's a flag over me in Spoon River.
A flag! A flag!

John Wasson

Oh! the dew-wet grass of the meadow in North Carolina
Through which Rebecca followed me wailing, wailing,
One child in her arms, and three that ran along wailing,
Lengthening out the farewell to me off to the war with the British,
And then the long, hard years down to the day of Yorktown.
And then my search for Rebecca,
Finding her at last in Virginia,
Two children dead in the meanwhile.
We went by oxen to Tennessee,
Thence after years to Illinois, 10
At last to Spoon River.
We cut the buffalo grass,
We felled the forests,
We built the schoolhouses, built the bridges,
Leveled the roads and tilled the fields
Alone with poverty, scourges, death –
If Harry Wilmans who fought the Filipinos
Is to have a flag on his grave,
Take it from mine.

Many Soldiers

The idea danced before us as a flag,
The sound of martial music,
The thrill of carrying a gun,
Advancement in the world on coming home,
A glint of glory, wrath for foes,
A dream of duty to country or to God.
But these were things in ourselves, shining before us,
They were not the power behind us,
Which was the Almighty hand of Life,
Like fire at earth's center making mountains,   10
Or pent-up waters that cut them through.
Do you remember the iron band
The blacksmith, Shack Dye, welded
Around the oak on Bennet's lawn,
From which to swing a hammock,
That daughter Janet might repose in, reading
On summer afternoons?
And that the growing tree at last
Sundered the iron band?
But not a cell in all the tree   20
Knew aught save that it thrilled with life,
Nor cared because the hammock fell
In the dust with Milton's *Poems*.

Harry Wilmans! You who fell in a swamp
Near Manila, following the flag,
You were not wounded by the greatness of a dream,
Or destroyed by ineffectual work,
Or driven to madness by Satanic snags.
You were not torn by aching nerves,
Nor did you carry great wounds to your old age.
You did not starve, for the government fed you.
You did not suffer yet cry 'forward'
To an army which you led   10
Against a foe with mocking smiles,
Sharper than bayonets. You were not smitten down
By invisible bombs. You were not rejected
By those for whom you were defeated.
You did not eat the savorless bread
Which a poor alchemy had made from ideals.
You went to Manila, Harry Wilmans,
While I enlisted in the bedraggled army
Of bright-eyed, divine youths,
Who surged forward, who were driven back and fell,   20
Sick, broken, crying, shorn of faith,
Following the flag of the Kingdom of Heaven.
You and I, Harry Wilmans, have fallen
In our several ways, not knowing
Good from bad, defeat from victory,
Nor what face it is that smiles
Behind the demoniac mask.

Lyman King

You may think, passer-by, that Fate
Is a pitfall outside of yourself,
Around which you may walk by the use of foresight
And wisdom.
Thus you believe, viewing the lives of other men,
As one who in godlike fashion bends over an anthill,
Seeing how their difficulties could be avoided.
But pass on into life:
In time you shall see Fate approach you
In the shape of your own image in the mirror,   10
Or you shall sit alone by your own hearth,
And suddenly the chair by you shall hold a guest,
And you shall know that guest
And read the authentic message of his eyes.

Caroline Branson

With our hearts like drifting suns, had we but walked,
As often before, the April fields till starlight
Silkened over with viewless gauze the darkness
Under the cliff, our trysting place in the wood,
Where the brook turns! Had we but passed from wooing
Like notes of music that run together, into winning,
In the inspired improvisation of love!
But to put back of us as a canticle ended
The rapt enchantment of the flesh,
In which our souls swooned, down, down,   10
Where time was not, nor space, nor ourselves –
Annihilated in love!
To leave these behind for a room with lamps:
And to stand with our Secret mocking itself,
And hiding itself amid flowers and mandolins,
Stared at by all between salad and coffee.
And to see him tremble, and feel myself
Prescient, as one who signs a bond –
Not flaming with gifts and pledges heaped
With rosy hands over his brow.   20
And then, O night! deliberate! unlovely!
With all of our wooing blotted out by the winning,
In a chosen room in an hour that was known to all!
Next day he sat so listless, almost cold,
So strangely changed, wondering why I wept,
Till a kind of sick despair and voluptuous madness
Seized us to make the pact of death.

A stalk of the earth-sphere,
Frail as starlight,
Waiting to be drawn once again   30
Into creation's stream.
But next time to be given birth,
Gazed at by Raphael and St Francis
Sometimes as they pass.
For I am their little brother,
To be known clearly face to face
Through a cycle of birth hereafter run.
You may know the seed and the soil,
You may feel the cold rain fall,
But only the earth-sphere, only heaven   40
Knows the secret of the seed
In the nuptial chamber under the soil.
Throw me into the stream again,
Give me another trial –
Save me, Shelley!

Anne Rutledge

Out of me unworthy and unknown
The vibrations of deathless music:
'With malice toward none, with charity for all.'
Out of me the forgiveness of millions toward millions,
And the beneficent face of a nation
Shining with justice and truth.
I am Anne Rutledge who sleep beneath these weeds,
Beloved in life of Abraham Lincoln,
Wedded to him, not through union,
But through separation.   10
Bloom forever, O Republic,
From the dust of my bosom!

Hamlet Micure

In a lingering fever many visions come to you:
I was in the little house again
With its great yard of clover
Running down to the board fence,
Shadowed by the oak tree,
Where we children had our swing.
Yet the little house was a manor hall
Set in a lawn, and by the lawn was the sea.
I was in the room where little Paul
Strangled from diphtheria,   10
But yet it was not this room –
It was a sunny verandah enclosed
With mullioned windows
And in a chair sat a man in a dark cloak
With a face like Euripides.
He had come to visit me, or I had gone to visit him –
I could not tell.
We could hear the beat of the sea, the clover nodded
Under a summer wind, and little Paul came
With clover blossoms to the window and smiled.   20
Then I said: 'What is "divine despair", Alfred?'
'Have you read "Tears, Idle Tears"?' he asked.
'Yes, but you do not there express divine despair.'
'My poor friend,' he answered, 'that was why the despair
Was divine.'

Mabel Osborne

Your red blossoms amid green leaves
Are drooping, beautiful geranium!
But you do not ask for water.
You cannot speak!
You do not need to speak –
Everyone knows that you are dying of thirst,
Yet they do not bring water!
They pass on, saying,
'The geranium wants water.'
And I, who had happiness to share   10
And longed to share your happiness;
I who loved you, Spoon River,
And craved your love,
Withered before your eyes, Spoon River –
Thirsting, thirsting,
Voiceless from chasteness of soul to ask you for love,
You who knew and saw me perish before you,
Like this geranium which someone has planted over me,
And left to die.

William H. Herndon

There by the window in the old house
Perched on the bluff, overlooking miles of valley,
My days of labor closed, sitting out life's decline,
Day by day did I look in my memory,
As one who gazes in an enchantress' crystal globe,
And I saw the figures of the past,
As if in a pageant glassed by a shining dream,
Move through the incredible sphere of time.
And I saw a man arise from the soil like a fabled giant[11]
And throw himself over a deathless destiny,   10
Master of great armies, head of the republic,
Bringing together into a dithyramb of recreative song
The epic hopes of a people;
At the same time Vulcan of sovereign fires,
Where imperishable shields and swords were beaten out
From spirits tempered in heaven.
Look in the crystal! See how he hastens on
To the place where his path comes up to the path
Of a child of Plutarch and Shakespeare.
O Lincoln, actor indeed, playing well your part,   20
And Booth[12], who strode in a mimic play within the play,
Often and often I saw you,
As the cawing crows winged their way to the wood
Over my housetop at solemn sunsets,
There by my window,
Alone.

Rutherford McDowell

They brought me ambrotypes
Of the old pioneers to enlarge.
And sometimes one sat for me –
Someone who was in being
When giant hands from the womb of the world
Tore the republic.
What was it in their eyes? –
For I could never fathom
That mystical pathos of drooped eyelids,
And the serene sorrow of their eyes.   10
It was like a pool of water,
Amid oak trees at the edge of a forest,
Where the leaves fall,
As you hear the crow of a cock
From a far-off farmhouse, seen near the hills
Where the third generation lives, and the strong men
And the strong women are gone and forgotten.
And these grandchildren and great-grandchildren
Of the pioneers!
Truly did my camera record their faces, too,   20
With so much of the old strength gone,
And the old faith gone,
And the old mastery of life gone,
And the old courage gone,
Which labors and loves and suffers and sings
Under the sun!

Hannah Armstrong

I wrote him a letter asking him for old times' sake
To discharge my sick boy from the army,
But maybe he couldn't read it.
Then I went to town and had James Garber,
Who wrote beautifully, write him a letter.
But maybe that was lost in the mails.
So I traveled all the way to Washington.
I was more than an hour finding the White House.
And when I found it they turned me away,
Hiding their smiles.   10
Then I thought:
'Oh, well, he ain't the same as when I boarded him
And he and my husband worked together
And all of us called him Abe, there in Menard.'
As a last attempt I turned to a guard and said:
'Please say it's old Aunt Hannah Armstrong
From Illinois, come to see him about her sick boy
In the army.'
Well, just in a moment they let me in!
And when he saw me he broke in a laugh,   20
And dropped his business as president,
And wrote in his own hand Doug's discharge,
Talking the while of the early days,
And telling stories.

Lucinda Matlock[13]

I went to the dances at Chandlerville,
And played snap-out at Winchester.
One time we changed partners,
Driving home in the moonlight of middle June,
And then I found Davis.
We were married and lived together for seventy years,
Enjoying, working, raising the twelve children,
Eight of whom we lost
Ere I had reached the age of sixty.
I spun, I wove, I kept the house, I nursed the sick,   10
I made the garden, and for holiday
Rambled over the fields where sang the larks,
And by Spoon River gathering many a shell,
And many a flower and medicinal weed –
Shouting to the wooded hills, singing to the green valleys.
At ninety-six I had lived enough, that is all,
And passed to a sweet repose.
What is this I hear of sorrow and weariness,
Anger, discontent and drooping hopes?
Degenerate sons and daughters,   20
Life is too strong for you –
It takes life to love Life.

Davis Matlock

Suppose it is nothing but the hive:
That there are drones and workers
And queens, and nothing but storing honey –
(Material things as well as culture and wisdom) –
For the next generation, this generation never living,
Except as it swarms in the sunlight of youth,
Strengthening its wings on what has been gathered,
And tasting, on the way to the hive
From the clover field, the delicate spoil.
Suppose all this, and suppose the truth: 10
That the nature of man is greater
Than nature's need in the hive;
And you must bear the burden of life,
As well as the urge from your spirit's excess –
Well, I say to live it out like a god
Sure of immortal life, though you are in doubt,
Is the way to live it.
If that doesn't make God proud of you
Then God is nothing but gravitation,
Or sleep is the golden goal.   20

Jennie M'Grew

Not, where the stairway turns in the dark,
A hooded figure, shriveled under a flowing cloak!
Not yellow eyes in the room at night,
Staring out from a surface of cobweb gray!
And not the flap of a condor wing,
When the roar of life in your ears begins
As a sound heard never before!
But on a sunny afternoon,
By a country road,
Where purple ragweeds bloom along a straggling fence,   10
And the field is gleaned, and the air is still,
To see against the sunlight something black,
Like a blot with an iris rim –
That is the sign to eyes of second sight…
And that I saw!

Columbus Cheney

This weeping willow!
Why do you not plant a few
For the millions of children not yet born,
As well as for us?
Are they not non-existent, or cells asleep
Without mind?
Or do they come to earth, their birth
Rupturing the memory of previous being?
Answer! The field of unexplored intuition is yours.
But in any case why not plant willows for them,   10
As well as for us?

Marie Bateson

You observe the carven hand
With the index finger pointing heavenward.
That is the direction, no doubt.
But how shall one follow it?
It is well to abstain from murder and lust,
To forgive, do good to others, worship God
Without graven images.
But these are external means after all
By which you chiefly do good to yourself.
The inner kernel is freedom,   10
It is light, purity –
I can no more.
Find the goal or lose it, according to your vision.

Tennessee Claflin Shope

I was the laughing-stock of the village,
Chiefly of the people of good sense, as they call themselves –
Also of the learned, like Revd Peet, who read Greek
The same as English.
For instead of talking free trade,
Or preaching some form of baptism,
Instead of believing in the efficacy
Of walking cracks, picking up pins the right way,
Seeing the new moon over the right shoulder,
Or curing rheumatism with blue glass,   10
I asserted the sovereignty of my own soul.
Before Mary Baker G. Eddy even got started
With what she called science
I had mastered the *Bhagavad-Gita*,
And cured my soul, before Mary
Began to cure bodies with souls –
Peace to all worlds!

Imanuel Ehrenhardt

I began with Sir William Hamilton's lectures.
Then studied Dugald Stewart;
And then John Locke on the Understanding,
And then Descartes, Fichte and Schelling,
Kant and then Schopenhauer –
Books I borrowed from old Judge Somers.
All read with rapturous industry
Hoping it was reserved to me
To grasp the tail of the ultimate secret,
And drag it out of its hole.   10
My soul flew up ten thousand miles
And only the moon looked a little bigger.
Then I fell back, how glad of the earth!
All through the soul of William Jones
Who showed me a letter of John Muir.

Samuel Gardner

I who kept the greenhouse,
Lover of trees and flowers,
Oft in life saw this umbrageous elm,
Measuring its generous branches with my eye,
And listened to its rejoicing leaves
Lovingly patting each other
With sweet aeolian whispers.
And well they might:
For the roots had grown so wide and deep
That the soil of the hill could not withhold   10
Aught of its virtue, enriched by rain,
And warmed by the sun,
But yielded it all to the thrifty roots,
Through which it was drawn and whirled to the trunk,
And thence to the branches, and into the leaves,
Wherefrom the breeze took life and sang.
Now I, an undertenant of the earth, can see
That the branches of a tree
Spread no wider than its roots.
And how shall the soul of a man   20
Be larger than the life he has lived?

Dow Kritt

Samuel is forever talking of his elm –
But I did not need to die to learn about roots:
I, who dug all the ditches about Spoon River.
Look at my elm!
Sprung from as good a seed as his,
Sown at the same time,
It is dying at the top:
Not from lack of life, nor fungus,
Nor destroying insect, as the sexton thinks.
Look, Samuel, where the roots have struck rock,   10
And can no further spread.
And all the while the top of the tree
Is tiring itself out, and dying,
Trying to grow.

William Jones

Once in a while a curious weed unknown to me,
Needing a name from my books,
Once in a while a letter from Yeomans.
Out of the mussel shells gathered along the shore
Sometimes a pearl with a glint like meadow rue:
Then betimes a letter from Tyndall in England,
Stamped with the stamp of Spoon River.
I, lover of Nature, beloved for my love of her,
Held such converse afar with the great
Who knew her better than I.   10
Oh, there is neither lesser nor greater,
Save as we make her greater and win from her keener delight.
With shells from the river cover me, cover me.
I lived in wonder, worshipping earth and heaven.
I have passed on the march eternal of endless life.

To all in the village I seemed, no doubt,
To go this way and that way, aimlessly.
But here by the river you can see at twilight
The soft-winged bats fly zig-zag here and there –
They must fly so to catch their food.
And if you have ever lost your way at night,
In the deep wood near Miller's Ford,
And dodged this way and now that,
Wherever the light of the Milky Way shone through,
Trying to find the path,   10
You should understand I sought the way
With earnest zeal, and all my wanderings
Were wanderings in the quest.

J. Milton Miles

Whenever the Presbyterian bell
Was rung by itself, I knew it as the Presbyterian bell.
But when its sound was mingled
With the sound of the Methodist, the Christian,
The Baptist and the Congregational,
I could no longer distinguish it,
Nor any one from the others, or either of them.
And as many voices called to me in life,
Marvel not that I could not tell
The true from the false,   10
Nor even, at last, the voice that I should have known.

Faith Matheny

At first you will know not what they mean,
And you may never know,
And we may never tell you –
These sudden flashes in your soul,
Like lambent lightning on snowy clouds
At midnight when the moon is full.
They come in solitude, or perhaps
You sit with your friend, and all at once
A silence falls on speech, and his eyes
Without a flicker glow at you: 10
You two have seen the secret together,
He sees it in you, and you in him.
And there you sit thrilling lest the Mystery
Stand before you and strike you dead
With a splendor like the sun's.
Be brave, all souls who have such visions!
As your body's alive as mine is dead,
You're catching a little whiff of the ether
Reserved for God Himself.

Willie Metcalf

I was Willie Metcalf.
They used to call me 'Dr Meyers',
Because, they said, I looked like him.
And he was my father, according to Jack McGuire.
I lived in the livery stable,
Sleeping on the floor
Side by side with Roger Baughman's bulldog,
Or sometimes in a stall.
I could crawl between the legs of the wildest horses
Without getting kicked – we knew each other.   10
 On spring days I tramped through the country
To get the feeling, which I sometimes lost,
That I was not a separate thing from the earth.
I used to lose myself, as if in sleep,
By lying with eyes half open in the woods.
Sometimes I talked with animals – even toads and snakes –
Anything that had an eye to look into.
Once I saw a stone in the sunshine
Trying to turn into jelly.
In April days in this cemetery   20
The dead people gathered all about me,
And grew still, like a congregation in silent prayer.
I never knew whether I was a part of the earth
With flowers growing in me, or whether I walked –
Now I know.

Willie Pennington

They called me the weakling, the simpleton,
For my brothers were strong and beautiful,
While I, the last child of parents who had aged,
Inherited only their residue of power.
But they, my brothers, were eaten up
In the fury of the flesh, which I had not,
Made pulp in the activity of the senses, which I had not,
Hardened by the growth of the lusts, which I had not,
Though making names and riches for themselves.
Then I, the weak one, the simpleton,   10
Resting in a little corner of life,
Saw a vision, and through me many saw the vision,
Not knowing it was through me.
Thus a tree sprang
From me, a mustard seed.[14]

The Village Atheist

Ye young debaters over the doctrine
Of the soul's immortality,
I who lie here was the village atheist,
Talkative, contentious, versed in the arguments
Of the infidels.
But through a long sickness
Coughing myself to death
I read the *Upanishads* and the poetry of Jesus.
And they lighted a torch of hope and intuition
And desire which the Shadow   10
Leading me swiftly through the caverns of darkness,
Could not extinguish.
Listen to me, ye who live in the senses
And think through the senses only:
Immortality is not a gift,
Immortality is an achievement,
And only those who strive mightily
Shall possess it.

John Ballard

In the lust of my strength
I cursed God, but he paid no attention to me:
I might as well have cursed the stars.
In my last sickness I was in agony, but I was resolute
And I cursed God for my suffering:
Still He paid no attention to me,
He left me alone, as He had always done.
I might as well have cursed the Presbyterian steeple.
Then, as I grew weaker, a terror came over me:
Perhaps I had alienated God by cursing him.   10
One day Lydia Humphrey brought me a bouquet
And it occurred to me to try to make friends with God,
So I tried to make friends with Him,
But I might as well have tried to make friends with the bouquet.
Now I was very close to the secret,
For I really could make friends with the bouquet
By holding close to me the love in me for the bouquet
And so I was creeping up on the secret, but –

Julian Scott

Toward the last
The truth of others was untruth to me,
The justice of others injustice to me,
Their reasons for death, reasons with me for life,
Their reasons for life, reasons with me for death.
I would have killed those they saved,
And saved those they killed.
And I saw how a god, if brought to earth,
Must act out what he saw and thought,
And could not live in this world of men   10
And act among them side by side
Without continual clashes.
The dust's for crawling, heaven's for flying –
Wherefore, O soul, whose wings are grown,
Soar upward to the sun!

Alfonso Churchill

They laughed at me as 'Prof. Moon',
As a boy in Spoon River, born with the thirst
Of knowing about the stars.
They jeered when I spoke of the lunar mountains,
And the thrilling heat and cold,
And the ebon valleys by silver peaks,
And Spica quadrillions of miles away,
And the littleness of man.
But now that my grave is honored, friends,
Let it not be because I taught   10
The lore of the stars in Knox College,
But rather for this: that through the stars
I preached the greatness of man,
Who is none the less a part of the scheme of things
For the distance of Spica or the Spiral Nebulae,
Nor any the less a part of the question
Of what the drama means.

Zilpha Marsh

At four o'clock in late October
I sat alone in the country schoolhouse
Back from the road, 'mid stricken fields,
And an eddy of wind blew leaves on the pane,
And crooned in the flue of the cannon-stove,
With its open door blurring the shadows
With the spectral glow of a dying fire.
In an idle mood I was running the planchette –
All at once my wrist grew limp,
And my hand moved rapidly over the board,   10
'Till the name of 'Charles Guiteau'[15] was spelled,
Who threatened to materialize before me.
I rose and fled from the room bare-headed
Into the dusk, afraid of my gift.
And after that the spirits swarmed –
Chaucer, Caesar, Poe and Marlowe,
Cleopatra and Mrs Surratt[16] –
Wherever I went, with messages, –
Mere trifling twaddle, Spoon River agreed.
You talk nonsense to children, don't you?   20
And suppose I see what you never saw
And never heard of and have no word for,
I must talk nonsense when you ask me
What it is I see!

Do you remember, passer-by, the path
I wore across the lot where now stands the opera house,
Hasting with swift feet to work through many years?
Take its meaning to heart:
You too may walk, after the hills at Miller's Ford
Seem no longer far away,
Long after you see them near at hand,
Beyond four miles of meadow;
And after woman's love is silent
Saying no more: 'I will save you.'   10
And after the faces of friends and kindred
Become as faded photographs, pitifully silent,
Sad for the look which means: 'We cannot help you.'
And after you no longer reproach mankind
With being in league against your soul's uplifted hands –
Themselves compelled at midnight and at noon
To watch with steadfast eye their destinies.
After you have these understandings, think of me
And of my path, who walked therein and knew
That neither man nor woman, neither toil,   20
Nor duty, gold nor power
Can ease the longing of the soul,
The loneliness of the soul!

Lydia Humphrey

Back and forth, back and forth, to and from the church,
With my Bible under my arm
'Till I was gray and old;
Unwedded, alone in the world,
Finding brothers and sisters in the congregation,
And children in the church.
I know they laughed and thought me queer.
I knew of the eagle souls that flew high in the sunlight,
Above the spire of the church, and laughed at the church,
Disdaining me, not seeing me. 10
But if the high air was sweet to them, sweet was the church to me.
It was the vision, vision, vision of the poets
Democratized!

Le Roy Goldman

'What will you do when you come to die,
If all your life long you have rejected Jesus,
And know as you lie there, He is not your friend?'
Over and over I said, I, the revivalist.
Ah, yes! but there are friends and friends.
And blessed are you, say I, who know all now,
You who have lost, ere you pass,
A father or mother, or old grandfather or mother,
Some beautiful soul that lived life strongly,
And knew you all through, and loved you ever,   10
Who would not fail to speak for you,
And give God an intimate view of your soul
As only one of your flesh could do it.
That is the hand your hand will reach for,
To lead you along the corridor
To the court where you are a stranger!

Gustav Richter

After a long day of work in my hothouses
Sleep was sweet, but if you sleep on your left side
Your dreams may be abruptly ended.
I was among my flowers where someone
Seemed to be raising them on trial,
As if after-while to be transplanted
To a larger garden of freer air.
And I was disembodied vision
Amid a light, as it were the sun
Had floated in and touched the roof of glass   10
Like a toy balloon and softly bursted,
And etherealized in golden air.
And all was silence, except the splendor
Was immanent with thought as clear
As a speaking voice, and I, as thought,
Could hear a Presence think as he walked
Between the boxes pinching off leaves,
Looking for bugs and noting values,
With an eye that saw it all:
'Homer, oh yes! Pericles, good.   20
Caesar Borgia, what shall be done with it?
Dante, too much manure, perhaps.
Napoleon, leave him awhile as yet.
Shelley, more soil. Shakespeare, needs spraying –'
Clouds, eh! –

Arlo Will

Did you ever see an alligator
Come up to the air from the mud,
Staring blindly under the full glare of noon?
Have you seen the stabled horses at night
Tremble and start back at the sight of a lantern?
Have you ever walked in darkness
When an unknown door was open before you
And you stood, it seemed, in the light of a thousand candles
Of delicate wax?
Have you walked with the wind in your ears   10
And the sunlight about you
And found it suddenly shine with an inner splendor?
Out of the mud many times,
Before many doors of light,
Through many fields of splendor,
Where around your steps a soundless glory scatters
Like new-fallen snow,
Will you go through earth, O strong of soul,
And through unnumbered heavens
To the final flame!   20

Captain Orlando Killion

Oh, you young radicals and dreamers,
You dauntless fledglings
Who pass by my headstone,
Mock not its record of my captaincy in the army
And my faith in God!
They are not denials of each other.
Go by reverently, and read with sober care
How a great people, riding with defiant shouts
The centaur of Revolution,
Spurred and whipped to frenzy,   10
Shook with terror, seeing the mist of the sea
Over the precipice they were nearing,
And fell from his back in precipitate awe
To celebrate the Feast of the Supreme Being.
Moved by the same sense of vast reality
Of life and death, and burdened as they were
With the fate of a race,
How was I, a little blasphemer,
Caught in the drift of a nation's unloosened flood,
To remain a blasphemer,   20
And a captain in the army?

Joseph Dixon

Who carved this shattered harp on my stone?
I died to you, no doubt. But how many harps and pianos
Wired I and tightened and disentangled for you,
Making them sweet again – with tuning fork or without?
Oh well! A harp leaps out of the ear of a man, you say,
But whence the ear that orders the length of the strings
To a magic of numbers flying before your thought
Through a door that closes against your breathless wonder?
Is there no Ear round the ear of a man, that it senses
Through strings and columns of air the soul of sound?   10
I thrill as I call it a tuning fork that catches
The waves of mingled music and light from afar,
The antennae of Thought that listens through utmost space.
Surely the concord that ruled my spirit is proof
Of an Ear that tuned me, able to tune me over
And use me again if I am worthy to use.

In the last spring I ever knew,
In those last days,
I sat in the forsaken orchard
Where beyond fields of greenery shimmered
The hills at Miller's Ford,
Just to muse on the apple tree
With its ruined trunk and blasted branches,
And shoots of green whose delicate blossoms
Were sprinkled over the skeleton tangle,
Never to grow in fruit.   10
And there was I with my spirit girded
By the flesh half dead, the senses numb,
Yet thinking of youth and the earth in youth, –
Such phantom blossoms palely shining
Over the lifeless boughs of Time.
O earth that leaves us ere heaven takes us!
Had I been only a tree to shiver
With dreams of spring and a leafy youth,
Then I had fallen in the cyclone
Which swept me out of the soul's suspense   20
Where it's neither earth nor heaven.

Aaron Hatfield

Better than granite, Spoon River,
Is the memory-picture you keep of me
Standing before the pioneer men and women
There at Concord Church on Communion day,
Speaking in broken voice of the peasant youth
Of Galilee who went to the city
And was killed by bankers and lawyers;
My voice mingling with the June wind
That blew over wheatfields from Atterbury,
While the white stones in the burying ground   10
Around the Church shimmered in the summer sun.
And there, though my own memories
Were too great to bear, were you, O pioneers,
With bowed heads breathing forth your sorrow
For the sons killed in battle and the daughters
And little children who vanished in life's morning,
Or at the intolerable hour of noon.
But in those moments of tragic silence,
When the wine and bread were passed,
Came the reconciliation for us –   20
Us the ploughmen and the hewers of wood,
Us the peasants, brothers of the peasant of Galilee –
To us came the Comforter
And the consolation of tongues of flame!

Isaiah Beethoven

They told me I had three months to live,
So I crept to Bernadotte,
And sat by the mill for hours and hours
Where the gathered waters deeply moving
Seemed not to move:
O world, that's you!
You are but a widened place in the river
Where Life looks down and we rejoice for her
Mirrored in us, and so we dream
And turn away, but when again   10
We look for the face, behold the lowlands
And blasted cottonwood trees where we empty
Into the larger stream!
But here by the mill the castled clouds
Mocked themselves in the dizzy water,
And over its agate floor at night
The flame of the moon ran under my eyes
Amid a forest stillness broken
By a flute in a hut on the hill.
At last when I came to lie in bed   20
Weak and in pain, with the dreams about me,
The soul of the river had entered my soul,
And the gathered power of my soul was moving
So swiftly it seemed to be at rest
Under cities of cloud and under
Spheres of silver and changing worlds –
Until I saw a flash of trumpets
Above the battlements over Time!

Elijah Browning

I was among multitudes of children
Dancing at the foot of a mountain.
A breeze blew out of the east and swept them as leaves,
Driving some up the slopes... All was changed.
Here were flying lights, and mystic moons, and dream-music.
A cloud fell upon us. When it lifted all was changed.
I was now amid multitudes who were wrangling.
Then a figure in shimmering gold, and one with a trumpet,
And one with a scepter stood before me.
They mocked me and danced a rigadoon and vanished...   10
All was changed again. Out of a bower of poppies
A woman bared her breasts and lifted her open mouth to mine.
I kissed her. The taste of her lips was like salt.
She left blood on my lips. I fell exhausted.
I arose and ascended higher, but a mist as from an iceberg
Clouded my steps. I was cold and in pain.
Then the sun streamed on me again,
And I saw the mists below me hiding all below them.
And I, bent over my staff, knew myself
Silhouetted against the snow. And above me   20
Was the soundless air, pierced by a cone of ice,
Over which hung a solitary star!
A shudder of ecstasy, a shudder of fear
Ran through me. But I could not return to the slopes –
Nay, I wished not to return.
For the spent waves of the symphony of freedom
Lapped the ethereal cliffs about me.
Therefore I climbed to the pinnacle.
I flung away my staff.
I touched that star   30
With my outstretched hand.
I vanished utterly.
For the mountain delivers to Infinite Truth
Whosoever touches the star!

Do you remember, O Delphic Apollo,
The sunset hour by the river, when Mickey M'Grew
Cried, 'There's a ghost,' and I, 'It's Delphic Apollo.'
And the son of the banker derided us, saying, 'It's light
By the flags at the water's edge, you half-witted fools,'
And from thence, as the wearisome years rolled on, long after
Poor Mickey fell down in the water tower to his death
Down, down, through bellowing darkness, I carried
The vision which perished with him like a rocket which falls
And quenches its light in earth, and hid it for fear   10
Of the son of the banker, calling on Plutus to save me?
Avenged were you for the shame of a fearful heart,
Who left me alone till I saw you again in an hour
When I seemed to be turned to a tree with trunk and branches
Growing indurate, turning to stone, yet burgeoning
In laurel leaves, in hosts of lambent laurel,
Quivering, fluttering, shrinking, fighting the numbness
Creeping into their veins from the dying trunk and branches!
'Tis vain, O youth, to fly the call of Apollo.
Fling yourselves in the fire, die with a song of spring,   20
If die you must in the spring. For none shall look
On the face of Apollo and live, and choose you must
'Twixt death in the flame and death after years of sorrow,
Rooted fast in the earth, feeling the grisly hand,
Not so much in the trunk as in the terrible numbness
Creeping up to the laurel leaves that never cease
To flourish until you fall. O leaves of me
Too sere for coronal wreaths, and fit alone
For urns of memory, treasured, perhaps, as themes
For hearts heroic, fearless singers and livers –   30
Delphic Apollo!

The Spooniad[17]

Of John Cabanis' wrath and of the strife
Of hostile parties, and his dire defeat
Who led the common people in the cause
Of freedom for Spoon River, and the fall
Of Rhodes' bank that brought unnumbered woes
And loss to many, with engendered hate
That flamed into the torch in Anarch hands
To burn the courthouse, on whose blackened wreck
A fairer temple rose and Progress stood –
Sing, Muse, that lit the Chian's face with smiles   10
Who saw the ant-like Greeks and Trojans crawl
About Scamander, over walls, pursued
Or else pursuing, and the funeral pyres
And sacred hecatombs, and first because
Of Helen who with Paris fled to Troy
As soulmate; and the wrath of Peleus' son,
Decreed to lose Chryseis, lovely spoil
Of war, and dearest concubine.
                              Say first,
Thou son of night, called Momus, from whose eyes   20
No secret hides, and Thalia, smiling one,
What bred 'twixt Thomas Rhodes and John Cabanis
The deadly strife? His daughter Flossie, she,
Returning from her wandering with a troop
Of strolling players, walked the village streets,
Her bracelets tinkling and with sparkling rings
And words of serpent wisdom and a smile
Of cunning in her eyes. Then Thomas Rhodes,
Who ruled the church and ruled the bank as well,
Made known his disapproval of the maid,   30
And all Spoon River whispered and the eyes
Of all the church frowned on her, till she knew
They feared her and condemned.
                              But them to flout

218

She gave a dance to viols and to flutes,
Brought from Peoria, and many youths,
But lately made regenerate through the prayers
Of zealous preachers and of earnest souls,
Danced merrily, and sought her in the dance,
Who wore a dress so low of neck that eyes   40
Down straying might survey the snowy swale
'Till it was lost in whiteness.
                              With the dance
The village changed to merriment from gloom.
The milliner, Mrs Williams, could not fill
Her orders for new hats, and every seamstress
Plied busy needles making gowns, old trunks
And chests were opened for their store of laces,
And rings and trinkets were brought out of hiding
And all the youths fastidious grew of dress,   50
Notes passed, and many a fair one's door at eve
Knew a bouquet, and strolling lovers thronged
About the hills that overlooked the river.
Then, since the mercy seats[17] more empty showed,
One of God's chosen lifted up his voice:
'The woman of Babylon is among us; rise
Ye sons of light and drive the wanton forth!'
So John Cabanis left the church and left
The hosts of law and order with his eyes
By anger cleared, and him the liberal cause   60
Acclaimed as nominee to the mayoralty
To vanquish A.D. Blood.
                              But as the war
Waged bitterly for votes and rumors flew
About the bank, and of the heavy loans
Which Rhodes' son had made to prop his loss
In wheat, and many drew their coin and left
The bank of Rhodes more hollow, with the talk
Among the liberals of another bank
Soon to be chartered, lo, the bubble burst   70

'Mid cries and curses, but the liberals laughed
And in the hall of Nicholas Bindle held
Wise converse and inspiriting debate.

High on a stage that overlooked the chairs
Where dozens sat, and where a pop-eyed daub
Of Shakespeare, very like the hired man
Of Christian Dallman, brow and pointed beard,
Upon a drab proscenium outward stared,
Sat Harmon Whitney, to that eminence,
By merit raised in ribaldry and guile,   80
And to the assembled rebels thus he spake:
'Whether to lie supine and let a clique
Cold-blooded, scheming, hungry, singing psalms,
Devour our substance, wreck our banks and drain
Our little hoards for hazards on the price
Of wheat or pork, or yet to cower beneath
The shadow of a spire upreared to curb
A breed of lackeys and to serve the bank
Coadjutor in greed, that is the question.
Shall we have music and the jocund dance,   90
Or tolling bells? Or shall young romance roam
These hills about the river, flowering now
To April's tears, or shall they sit at home,
Or play croquet where Thomas Rhodes may see,
I ask you? If the blood of youth runs o'er
And riots 'gainst this regimen of gloom,
Shall we submit to have these youths and maids
Branded as libertines and wantons?'
                                          Ere
His words were done a woman's voice called 'No!'   100
Then rose a sound of moving chairs, as when
The numerous swine o'er-run the replenished troughs,
And every head was turned, as when a flock
Of geese back-turning to the hunter's tread
Rise up with flapping wings. Then rang the hall

With riotous laughter, for with battered hat
Tilted upon her saucy head, and fist
Raised in defiance, Daisy Fraser stood.
Headlong she had been hurled from out the hall
Save Wendell Bloyd, who spoke for woman's rights,   110
Prevented, and the bellowing voice of Burchard.
Then 'mid applause she hastened toward the stage
And flung both gold and silver to the cause
And swiftly left the hall.
                                    Meantime upstood
A giant figure, bearded like the son
Of Alcmene, deep-chested, round of paunch,
And spoke in thunder: 'Over there behold
A man who for the truth withstood his wife –
Such is our spirit – when that A.D. Blood   120
Compelled me to remove Dom Pedro –'
                                    Quick
Before Jim Brown could finish, Jefferson Howard
Obtained the floor and spake: 'Ill suits the time
For clownish words, and trivial is our cause
If naught's at stake but John Cabanis' wrath,
He who was erstwhile of the other side
And came to us for vengeance. More's at stake
Than triumph for New England or Virginia.
And whether rum be sold, or for two years   130
As in the past two years, this town be dry
Matters but little – Oh yes, revenue
For sidewalks, sewers, that is well enough!
I wish to God this fight were now inspired
By other passion than to salve the pride
Of John Cabanis or his daughter. Why
Can never contests of great moment spring
From worthy things, not little? Still, if men
Must always act so, and if rum must be
The symbol and the medium to release   140
From life's denial and from slavery,

Then give me rum!'
                    Exultant cries arose.
Then, as George Trimble had o'ercome his fear
And vacillation and begun to speak,
The door creaked and the idiot, Willie Metcalf,
Breathless and hatless, whiter than a sheet,
Entered and cried: 'The marshal's on his way
To arrest you all. And if you only knew
Who's coming here tomorrow – I was listening   150
Beneath the window where the other side
Are making plans.'
                    So to a smaller room
To hear the idiot's secret some withdrew
Selected by the Chair: the Chair himself
And Jefferson Howard, Benjamin Pantier,
And Wendell Bloyd, George Trimble, Adam Weirauch,
Imanuel Ehrenhardt, Seth Compton, Godwin James
And Enoch Dunlap, Hiram Scates, Roy Butler,
Carl Hamblin, Roger Heston, Ernest Hyde   160
And Penniwit, the artist, Kinsey Keene,
And E.C. Culbertson and Franklin Jones,
Benjamin Fraser, son of Benjamin Pantier
By Daisy Fraser, some of lesser note,
And secretly conferred.
                    But in the hall
Disorder reigned and when the marshal came
And found it so, he marched the hoodlums out
And locked them up.
                    Meanwhile within a room   170
Back in the basement of the church, with Blood
Counseled the wisest heads. Judge Somers first,
Deep learned in life, and next him, Elliott Hawkins
And Lambert Hutchins; next him Thomas Rhodes
And Editor Whedon; next him Garrison Standard,
A traitor to the liberals, who with lip
Upcurled in scorn and with a bitter sneer:

'Such strife about an insult to a woman –
A girl of eighteen' – Christian Dallman too,
And others unrecorded. Some there were   180
Who frowned not on the cup but loathed the rule
Democracy achieved thereby, the freedom
And lust of life it symbolized.

Now morn with snowy fingers up the sky
Flung like an orange at a festival
The ruddy sun, when from their hasty beds
Poured forth the hostile forces, and the streets
Resounded to the rattle of the wheels,
That drove this way and that to gather in
The tardy voters, and the cries of chieftains   190
Who manned the battle. But at ten o'clock
The liberals bellowed fraud, and at the polls
The rival candidates growled and came to blows.
Then proved the idiot's tale of yester-eve
A word of warning. Suddenly on the streets
Walked hog-eyed Allen, terror of the hills
That looked on Bernadotte ten miles removed.
No man of this degenerate day could lift
The boulders which he threw, and when he spoke
The windows rattled, and beneath his brows,   200
Thatched like a shed with bristling hair of black,
His small eyes glistened like a maddened boar.
And as he walked the boards creaked, as he walked
A song of menace rumbled. Thus he came,
The champion of A.D. Blood, commissioned
To terrify the liberals. Many fled
As when a hawk soars o'er the chicken yard.
He passed the polls and with a playful hand
Touched Brown, the giant, and he fell against,
As though he were a child, the wall, so strong   210
Was hog-eyed Allen. But the liberals smiled.
For soon as hog-eyed Allen reached the walk,

Close on his steps paced Bengal Mike, brought in
By Kinsey Keene, the subtle-witted one,
To match the hog-eyed Allen. He was scarce
Three-fourths the other's bulk, but steel his arms,
And with a tiger's heart. Two men he killed
And many wounded in the days before,
And no one feared.

               But when the hog-eyed one   220
Saw Bengal Mike his countenance grew dark,
The bristles o'er his red eyes twitched with rage,
The song he rumbled lowered. Round and round
The courthouse paced he, followed stealthily
By Bengal Mike, who jeered him every step:
'Come, elephant, and fight! Come, hog-eyed coward!
Come, face about and fight me, lumbering sneak!
Come, beefy bully, hit me, if you can!
Take out your gun, you duffer, give me reason
To draw and kill you. Take your billy out.   230
I'll crack your boar's head with a piece of brick!'
But never a word the hog-eyed one returned
But trod about the courthouse, followed both
By troops of boys and watched by all the men.
All day, they walked the square. But when Apollo
Stood with reluctant look above the hills
As fain to see the end, and all the votes
Were cast, and closed the polls, before the door
Of Trainor's drugstore Bengal Mike, in tones
That echoed through the village, bawled the taunt: 240
'Who was your mother, hog-eyed?' In a trice,
As when a wild boar turns upon the hound
That through the brakes upon an August day
Has gashed him with its teeth, the hog-eyed one
Rushed with his giant arms on Bengal Mike
And grabbed him by the throat. Then rose to heaven
The frightened cries of boys, and yells of men
Forth rushing to the street. And Bengal Mike

Moved this way and now that, drew in his head
As if his neck to shorten, and bent down   250
To break the death grip of the hog-eyed one,
'Twixt guttural wrath and fast-expiring strength
Striking his fists against the invulnerable chest
Of hog-eyed Allen. Then, when some came in
To part them, others stayed them, and the fight
Spread among dozens; many valiant souls
Went down from clubs and bricks.

                             But tell me, Muse,
What god or goddess rescued Bengal Mike?
With one last, mighty struggle did he grasp   260
The murderous hands and turning kick his foe.
Then, as if struck by lightning, vanished all
The strength from hog-eyed Allen, at his side
Sank limp those giant arms and o'er his face
Dread pallor and the sweat of anguish spread.
And those great knees, invincible but late,
Shook to his weight. And quickly as the lion
Leaps on its wounded prey, did Bengal Mike
Smite with a rock the temple of his foe,
And down he sank and darkness o'er his eyes   270
Passed like a cloud.

                    As when the woodman fells
Some giant oak upon a summer's day
And all the songsters of the forest shrill,
And one great hawk that has his nestling young
Amid the topmost branches croaks, as crash
The leafy branches through the tangled boughs
Of brother oaks, so fell the hog-eyed one
Amid the lamentations of the friends
Of A.D. Blood.   280

             Just then, four lusty men
Bore the town marshal, on whose iron face
The purple pall of death already lay,
To Trainor's drug store, shot by Jack McGuire.

And cries went up of 'Lynch him!' and the sound
Of running feet from every side was heard
Bent on the

NOTES

1. From Lord Byron's *Childe Harold's Pilgrimage* (1812), Canto IV, stanza 179.

2. 'Science' here must mean Christian Science.

3. John Peter Altgeld (1847–1902) was a liberal, reformist governor of Illinois admired by Masters, who mentions him several times in the *Anthology*. Philip Armour (1832–1901) headed a leading meat-packing company in Chicago – not the sort of figure Masters admired.

4. Title character of the 1866 play *Brand* by Henrik Ibsen (1828–1906), Norwegian playwright.

5. John B. Alden (1827–1924) produced informational works like *Alden's Home Atlas of the World* (1888) and *Alden's Cyclopedia of Eminent Biography* (1892) as well as collections of poetry and prose. (Hallwas, *Annotated Edition*, p. 405.)

6. Cyclops, mythological race of one-eyed giants.

7. Millenium: 'a period of general righteousness and happiness, esp. in the indefinite future' (*The New Century Dictionary*, 1927).

8. An American labour organisation with highly idealistic aims and methods, which was active and influential in the last third of the nineteenth century.

9. The two titles in each pair contrast sharply: an eighteenth-century religious sceptic against an apologist for religion, and a nineteenth-century tragedy against a sentimental love story respectively.

10. According to Kimball Flaccus, the story in this poem reflects Masters' discovery of Shelley through a beautifully decorated book he bought shortly after graduating from high school. (Hallwas, *Annotated Edition*, p. 412.)

11. President Abraham Lincoln, whose biography Masters wrote after reading that by William H. Herndon (1818–91), Lincoln's last law partner.

12. John Wilkes Booth (1838–65) was the Southern-sympathising actor who assassinated Lincoln.

13. Lucinda and Davis Matlock are based on Masters' paternal grandparents, Lucinda and Davis Masters. 'Matlock' was his grandfather's mother's surname.

14. Referring to the parable reported in Matthew 13:31–2, Mark 4:31, and Luke 13:19.

15. Charles Guiteau (1840–82) was hanged for assassinating President James Garfield in 1881.

16. Mary E. Surratt (1820–65) was convicted and hanged as a member of the conspiracy to assassinate Lincoln.

17. This aborted mock epic involving a dispute over prohibition of the sale of alcohol in Spoon River was preceded by the following note in the first edition of the book:

[*The late Mr Jonathan Swift Somers, laureate of Spoon River, planned* The Spooniad *as an epic in twenty-four books, but unfortunately did not live to complete even the first book. The fragment was found among his papers by William Marion Reedy and was for the first time published in* Reedy's Mirror *of December 18th, 1914.*]

18. Mercy seat: 'the gold covering on the ark of the covenant, regarded as the resting place of God' (*The New Century Dictionary*, 1927).

LIST OF CHARACTER NAMES

Armstrong, Hannah
Arnett, Harold
Atherton, Lucius

Ballard, John
Barker, Amanda
Barrett, Pauline
Bartlett, Ezra
Bateson, Marie
Beatty, Tom
Beethoven, Isaiah
Bennett, Hon. Henry
Bindle, Nicholas
Blind Jack
Bliss, Mrs Charles
Blood, A.D.
Bloyd, Wendell P.
Bone, Richard
Branson, Caroline
Brown, Jim
Brown, Sarah
Browning, Elijah
Burleson, John Horace
Butler, Roy

Cabanis, Flossie
Calhoun, Granville
Calhoun, Henry C.
Campbell, Calvin
Carman, Eugene
Cheney, Columbus
Childers, Elizabeth
Church, John M.
Churchill, Alfonso

Circuit Judge, The
Clapp, Homer
Clark, Nellie
Clute, Aner
Compton, Conant Seth, Edith
Culbertson, E.C.

Davidson, Robert
Dement, Silas
Dixon, Joseph
Drummer, Frank
Drummer, Hare
Dunlap, Enoch
Dye, Shack

Ehrenhardt, Imanuel

Fallas, State's Attorney
Fawcett, Clarence
Fluke, Willard
Foote, Searcy
Ford, Webster
Fraser, Benjamin
Fraser, Daisy
French, Charlie
Frickey, Ida

Garber, James
Gardner, Samuel
Garrick, Amelia
Godbey, Jacob
Goldman, Le Roy
Goode, William
Goodpasture, Jacob

Graham, Magrady
Gray, George
Green, Ami
Greene, Hamilton
Griffy the Cooper
Gustine, Dorcas

Hainsfeather, Barney
Hamblin, Carl
Hatfield, Aaron
Hawkins, Elliott
Hawley, Jeduthan
Henry, Chase
Herndon, William H.
Heston, Roger
Higbie, Archibald
Hill, Doc
Hoheimer, Knowlt
Holden, Barry
Hookey, Sam
Howard, Jefferson
Hueffer, Cassius
Hummel, Oscar
Humphrey, Lydia
Hutchins, Lambert
Hyde, Ernest

James, Godwin
Jones, Fiddler
Jones, Franklin
Jones, 'Indignation'
Jones, Minerva
Jones, William

Karr, Elmer
Keene, Jonas

Kessler, Bert
Kessler, Mrs
Killion, Captain Orlando
Kincaid, Russell
King, Lyman
Knapp, Nancy
Konovaloff, Ippolit
Kritt, Dow

Layton, Henry

M'Cumber, Daniel
McDowell, Rutherford
McFarlane, Widow
McGee, Fletcher
McGee, Ollie
M'Grew, Jennie
M'Grew, Mickey
McGuire, Jack
McNeely, Mary
McNeely, Washington
Malloy, Father
Many Soldiers
Marsh, Zilpha
Marshall, Herbert
Mason, Serepta
Matheny, Faith
Matlock, Davis
Matlock, Lucinda
Melveny, Abel
Merritt, Mrs
Merritt, Tom
Metcalf, Willie
Meyers, Dr
Meyers, Mrs
Micure, Hamlet

INDEX OF TITLES AND FIRST LINES

Edgar Lee Masters was born in Garnett, Kansas on 23rd August 1868. The son of Hardin Wallace Masters, a lawyer, and Emma J. Dexter, he grew up in western Illinois on his grandfather's farm; this early experience of rural life went on to shape his writing. His literary aspirations were not encouraged by his father, and having been educated in public schools in Petersburg and Illinois, he read law, and founded a legal practice with Kicksham Scanlon in 1893.

Over the next ten years he wrote essays and plays, and in 1898, the same year that his first collection, *A Book of Verses*, was published, he married Helen M. Jenkins, with whom he had three children. In 1903 he joined Clarence Darrow's law firm, where he defended the poor, and continued writing poems and plays in his spare time. But his personal and professional life became unsettled, and he went into practice on his own in 1911.

In 1914 he began writing the poems that led to the *Spoon River Anthology* (published in 1915). The work was partly inspired by J.W. Mackail's *Selected Epigrams from the Greek Anthology*, and drew on his childhood background. It was an immediate popular and critical success, running through several editions rapidly, and drawing praise from John Cowper Powys, who called Masters 'the natural child of Walt Whitman', and Ezra Pound, who said 'at last, America has discovered a poet'. He continued to write poetry, novels, essays and biographies for nearly thirty years after this, but none equalled the success of *Spoon River Anthology*.

He left his family in 1917, moved to New York in 1920, divorced his wife after travelling to Europe in 1921, and married Ellen Coyne, a woman thirty years his junior, in 1926. While trying to balance his two careers of lawyer and writer, overwork led to a long-lasting and almost fatal attack of pneumonia. After his great literary success, the number of his legal clients had started to decrease, partly because some of the poems in *Spoon River Anthology* caused controversy with tales of bigotry and liaisons (it has been said that *Spoon River* was Masters' revenge on narrow-mindedness and hypocrisy). After marrying Coyne, Masters retired, devoting himself exclusively to writing. Throughout the 1940s he received major literary awards, such as the Poetry Society of America medal, the Shelley Memorial Award and the Academy of American Poets Fellowship. He died on 5th March 1950, and was buried in Oakland Cemetery in Petersburg, Illinois.

John Ridland has taught literature and writing at the University of California, Santa Barbara, since 1961. He has published books of poetry including *Ode on Violence*, *In the Shadowless Light*, *Elegy for my Aunt*, *Palms*, and *Life with Unkie*. He has previously translated *John the Valiant* from the Hungarian for Hesperus, and has received the Árpád Gold Medal from the Hungarian Congress in Cleveland for his contributions to Hungarian literature.

SELECTED TITLES FROM HESPERUS PRESS

Author	Title	Foreword writer
Jane Austen	*Love and Friendship*	Fay Weldon
Charlotte Brontë	*The Green Dwarf*	Libby Purves
Emily Brontë	*Poems of Solitude*	Helen Dunmore
Geoffrey Chaucer	*The Parliament of Birds*	
Anton Chekhov	*Three Years*	William Fiennes
Wilkie Collins	*Who Killed Zebedee?*	Martin Jarvis
William Congreve	*Incognita*	Peter Ackroyd
Joseph Conrad	*The Return*	Colm Tóibín
Charles Dickens	*The Haunted House*	Peter Ackroyd
Fyodor Dostoevsky	*The Double*	Jeremy Dyson
George Eliot	*Amos Barton*	Matthew Sweet
Henry Fielding	*Jonathan Wild the Great*	Peter Ackroyd
F. Scott Fitzgerald	*The Rich Boy*	John Updike
E.M. Forster	*Arctic Summer*	Anita Desai
Elizabeth Gaskell	*Lois the Witch*	Jenny Uglow
Thomas Hardy	*Fellow-Townsmen*	Emma Tennant
L.P. Hartley	*Simonetta Perkins*	Margaret Drabble
Nathaniel Hawthorne	*Rappaccini's Daughter*	Simon Schama
John Keats	*Fugitive Poems*	Andrew Motion
D.H. Lawrence	*Daughters of the Vicar*	Anita Desai
Katherine Mansfield	*In a German Pension*	Linda Grant
Prosper Mérimée	*Carmen*	Philip Pullman
Sándor Petőfi	*John the Valiant*	George Szirtes
Alexander Pope	*The Rape of the Lock*	Peter Ackroyd
Robert Louis Stevenson	*Dr Jekyll and Mr Hyde*	Helen Dunmore
Leo Tolstoy	*Hadji Murat*	Colm Tóibín
Mark Twain	*Tom Sawyer, Detective*	
Oscar Wilde	*The Portrait of Mr W.H.*	Peter Ackroyd
Virginia Woolf	*Carlyle's House and Other Sketches*	Doris Lessing